MW01287219

THE HAPHAZARD SERENDIPITOUS EASTER EGG HUNT

NICOLE ANDRES

ISBN 978-1-7160-5992-6

Copyright © 2021 by Nicole Andres

All rights reserved, including the right of reproduction in any form, or by any mechanical or electronic means including photocopying or recording, or by any information storage or retrieval system, in whole or in part in any form, and in any case not without the written permission of the author and publisher.

Disclaimer: This book is a memoir. It reflects the author's present recollections to the best of her knowledge of real experiences over time. Some names, places, and times have been changed to protect the privacy of individuals. The events in this book do not necessarily occur in the exact order as presented and may be compressed. The events described serve no harmful intention but are used instead by the author as deemed necessary to express and support personal opinions and values influenced by the experiences and events described herein.

Scripture texts in this work are taken from the New American Bible, revised edition © 1986 Confraternity of Christian Doctrine, Washington, D.C. and are used by permission of the copyright owner. All Rights Reserved. No part of the New American Bible may be reproduced in any form without permission in writing from the copyright owner.

Author website: facebook.com/NicoleAndres.writer

Published March 2021

DEDICATION

To: Mom, Dad, and Albert

TABLE OF CONTENTS

INTRODUCTION

✏

Sloppy Seconds, and Thirds...

Shoot for the stars! At least that's what they say. When I began writing this book, I was inspired and on a high of pursuing a dream. I was ready to document all of it so my success story would inspire readers everywhere. With a bow and arrow in my hands, I was aiming for the moon! I'm pretty sure I shot the neighbor's cat instead.

So, what started out as a journal to show off my success story, quickly became a journal for me to mentally work through sloppy servings of humble pie and real life - a mental walk through second chances, third chances, and endless new beginnings. Endless beginnings are like poetic blessings. This book doesn't follow a chronological success story that I planned perfectly in my head. Instead, the book follows the more valuable lessons learned not solely from failure but from what I often call "redirection." I'm hoping that all this redirection is keeping me on the right path. Of course, staying on the right path can be hard.

No Uber for Heaven

You see, I'm really just trying to get to Heaven, but right now I'm sitting in a little cafe to write this introduction, and out of nowhere I get distracted. It isn't due to the clanging of dishes, the banging and beeping of the register opening and closing, or the bustling of people in and out to grab their morning pick-me-up. Instead, I'm distracted by an outrageously HOT guy sitting about 20 feet in front of me. Just like that, my entire ability to focus is thrown off course. I have a gut feeling that there is approximately a 0.05 percent chance that anything will happen between this guy and me. In the words of Lloyd from the movie *Dumb and Dumber*, "So, you're telling me there's a chance?" Hey, there is a truth to Lloyd's optimism. Where there is a little faith, there is ALWAYS a chance.

As I've come to find out, there is some work involved when your goal is Heaven. Holding onto your faith during what feels like the least hopeful of times is a large chunk of that work. Whether I manage to land "Prince Charming" sitting across from me, land an average Joe, or stick with Finny (my pet fish), I'm pretty sure there is always more to it. Life itself hands you enough adventures filled with as many "warm fuzzies," as heartbreaks, and as many tough decisions as "no-brainers." We all daydream about being a superhero of sorts, be it a Ninja Turtle, or World's Best Mom/Dad. We all want to be successful in something. There's nothing wrong with that. Why is my goal Heaven?

Well, what do I do when my temper, patience, or faith is tested? Simple. I bow my head while I turn my thoughts to God. I might do it while cursing in anger, or tearing up from heartbreak, but I also do it in a peaceful calm and when jumping for joy. I have realized that regardless of my situation, Heaven is always where I end up looking. Therefore, why shouldn't Heaven just be my ultimate goal?

As I navigate through my mid-30's, there are days I feel young and I want to do a zillion things— travel, be a superhero, fall in love. Then there are days I feel old and grumpy and want nothing more than to drop dead and be done with the craziness of the world. However, if one awesome day happens and gives me a glimpse of hope in my dreams, I'm back on the naive young-adult dream-chasing bandwagon.

You'll come to find in the pages of this book that I try to pursue a lot of different goals including goals

I never even thought would cross my mind. I simply like to try different things, and I say why the heck not? People talk about ambition and trying new things as being a way great way to live your life, and yet many people either choose not to do it, or circumstances limit their chances. While reality may prove that to be true, I like to refer to words that legendary martial artist Bruce Lee used to say. As described by Linda Lee Cadwell, who was his wife, *"Circumstances?" he would say with a smile, "Hell, I make circumstances!"* Linda pointed out that Bruce never allowed adversity to throw him off course.[1] I believe that if you adopt his outlook, then possibilities are endless!

Most people have a bucket list, but I have (what I will talk about in another chapter) something I call a "backwards" bucket list." Instead of *writing* my list, I kind of stumbled upon it the more that my goals kept slipping through my fingers. This backwards bucket list manifests itself when you open your eyes to the lessons and accomplishments encountered while in pursuit of your goals. If you live more open to the possibility of failing, then every time you look back, you realize you have done ridiculous things the entire time you were just "trying to get yourself back on track." If you keep your eyes and mind open, you'll find that opportunities are scattered everywhere like some great Easter egg hunt. I'm not saying to live *completely* carelessly and without any kind of plan. That's not a bright idea. Rather, have a plan and don't be afraid of unplanned deviations. It's a matter of trusting God's will and accepting that while not all eggs you choose to pursue on your hunt hold the prize you envisioned, every egg contains something within. It's what I like to call the "Haphazard Serendipitous Easter Egg Hunt."

Another reason my goal is Heaven is that no matter what I accomplish or how badly I fall on my face, if I wake up the next day, I realize I've got to find some way to expand on the accomplishment or the fall. Whether in extreme joy or distress from the day before, it is all behind me. But when your time is up, then what? I don't necessarily mean this as a "go examine your conscience," alarm, but haven't you ever wondered what happens next? I don't think you can just Uber your way to Heaven.

Tattoos and Life Goals

To desire Heaven, kind of starts off like wanting a tattoo. Stay with me here. I've got a tattoo that I started wanting when I was around a sophomore in college. Knowing it would be permanent, I decided that maybe I should not get one. However, even a few years down the road, I realized I STILL contemplated a tattoo. Taking extreme care to develop and pick a tattoo design I would not regret, I followed through and finally got one. The key there was a design I would *not regret*. You see, the feeling of regret is probably my biggest fear. But back to getting the tattoo...

That evening, I walked down the sidewalk in the middle of downtown Greensboro, North Carolina. I grew more excited as I approached the tattoo parlor embedded along the shops and restaurants that lined the busy street. I never realized how much the parlor/ art shop visually added to the street itself. I never paid attention until now.

"Dude, this is crazy, but this is going to be so awesome," I told my friend who came along for moral support. He may have come more to see if I would follow through or scream in pain, but whatever, I was excited! Colors, swirls, and pictures of all kinds brightened the windows as I strolled along toward the entrance. From that point on, it was not the fear of the needle, it was the fear of what my dad would say. Maybe I was dumb enough to get a tattoo, but I wasn't dumb enough to tell my dad until AFTER it was completed. Naturally, my dad's initial reaction was silence.

"Look!" I desperately tried to save myself when dad found out. "I even made sure my design was special. See?" I insisted, pointing to the tattoo. "It's the cross from the picture on the front of the prayer card that Mom always showed us." My dad still didn't say anything. I'll leave it at that.

You'll find that no matter where my journeys take me, the only constant has been my faith. Whether in different classrooms, different states, or different countries, the challenges of change always bring me back to conversations with God. Now, a tattoo is nowhere NEAR the level of Heaven, but you get the idea. Like wanting that tattoo, wanting to go to Heaven is always present in my mind. I know that in the end, if I make good decisions and God-willing I get through the gates, I will not regret it. I've yet to look at my tattoo and wish it was not there. How much greater will Heaven be?

Having faith is the greatest gift my mother passed on to me. I have to say that God has pulled me through quite a bit! He sure must have a special kind of love because I'm pretty sure like my dad, God often stares at me in silence when I make some dumb decision. I don't know if God looks anything like this good-looking guy sitting across from me in the cafe, but at least I know God is the ultimate example of unconditional love. As tempting as Prince Charming 20 feet in front of me might be at this moment, it's probably wiser to chase after God first.

While I struggle as much as the next person "figuring life out" and I'm constantly distracted, I'm also learning how *not* to let the distractions (whether attractive or off-putting) get in the way of my path. In writing this book, I've found that while distractions haven't STOPPED me, I sure as heck have been on the least direct path known to man! But hey, progress is progress, and 0.05 percent is still a chance . . .

Super Short Summary and History

I was a teacher for almost seven years. My graduate degree is in special education, with a concentration in behavioral and emotional disorders. A majority of my teaching career was in the alternative setting, and to be truthful, I love teaching. Of all the careers I've pursued, I truly find teaching the best! I also send a shout out to teachers of all kinds everywhere! Unfortunately, working in a school (no matter how many I tried) just didn't fit how I knew *I* could help students. Simply put, I knew I had to get out of the career. Otherwise, I was going to end up as that "crabby teacher" whose only lasting effect was giving students things to laugh about when they were older, or worse, to cry about.

I took a leap of faith in changing my career. The chain of careers looks something like this: Prior to getting my degree in education, I studied a few semesters to be an architect. I ended up teaching. After that, I started small, trying tutoring, became ambitious and started to develop a martial arts program. Then I veered off and spent a year as a rookie volunteer firefighter, completed paramedic school, only to fail the most important lab exam to get into clinicals as a physical therapist assistant

(PTA) student. My hard-earned "emergency fund," slowly dwindled with each change. So much for chasing the dream. However, my story is anything but over! All this happened between 18 and now, my mid-30s.

So, here I am, living back at home. Tough pill of pride to swallow? Absolutely. Giving up? Not a chance.

A Weird but Undeniable Sense of Peace

Despite the uncertainty of my path, there is a weird sense of peace within me. I have no regrets, and while frustration and anger are often my company in my journey, so too is my faith. I am a Catholic, born, raised, and still practicing. My goal in sharing my stories is not to shove my religious beliefs in anyone's face. However, as I wrote about each event, I realized that without consciously trying, my faith always made its way into each story. This phenomenon became even more profound toward the end of the book. Once that became apparent, I decided that to leave my faith out of my writing would simply be an insult to what God has done for me. He has pulled me through this far, kept me protected and well provided for. God has remained faithful to me…seems a bit paradoxical, but it sure does prove how strong his love is. I find it important to include showing how much of a role my faith has played in my life. So rather than try to write around it, I will share it as it naturally makes its way into each chapter.

The events I share are intended for *anyone and everyone* to read. I'm confident enough to say that my faith is strong, but I'm also human enough to admit that the many times I have just barely pulled through, my survival has been made possible by the weakest hint of faith I could find within. I encourage my readers to approach my book with an open mind and realize that whether or not you are a believer in Christ, I'm willing to bet that you will relate to at least one section of this book. In doing so, I hope to at least give you some encouragement or hope to keep tucked away for a rainy day.

So, let's get going, shall we?

Let's Get Some Things Straight: A Few Disclaimers

♪

Every person has experiences unique to them. These are simply some of my experiences and thoughts along the way. I just hope to encourage you wherever you may be in life.

This book is a memoir. It reflects the author's present recollections to the best of her knowledge of real experiences over time. Some names, places, and times have been changed to protect the privacy of individuals. The events in this book do not necessarily occur in the exact order as presented and may be compressed. The events described serve no harmful intention but are used instead by the author as deemed necessary to express and support personal opinions and values influenced by the experiences and events described herein.

1

COFFEE-INDUCED
REVELATIONS

Coffee Shops

I have never been one to hang out at coffee shops, and other than the smell of coffee, I often choose tea over coffee. Ironically, as I began to delve into writing this book, I found myself spending more time in coffee shops, whether in a Barnes and Noble or in little "nooks" and local businesses. Naturally, I developed the ability to tune out the noise of whirring machines, loud clinking of cups, and the variety of music that played at each place. As the noises became easier to ignore, another sound caught my ear. This sound became one of many examples of my saving grace. The sounds of confusion and worry led me to the revelation that no one has their life together. At least, not in a storybook-ending kind of way.

A Little Background

About eight months prior to beginning this memoir, I left my job as a teacher. It was time for me to initiate a change. Upon leaving the job, I took my "mental break" from the career. I read more books, exercised more, and even painted. I became a volunteer firefighter, in hopes that it might lead me into a new career. Being able to do so many things was a blessing.

As I continued to live out this "sort of" vacation, I had to face reality. My income was next to nothing. I was living off emergency money, and although I anticipated that, it was never part of my permanent plan. I knew I still desired to LIVE my life, not simply cruise along. Hoping it would financially help me scrape up some money and get me going, I picked up a tutoring job at a place I ended up not liking. However, beggars cannot be choosy, and I was determined to stick it out until I could find something else. It did not take long to become angry as I constantly wondered why no one else would hire me, despite a decent resume. Disheartened, I began to sense that my situation was not going to get any better. I racked my brain every second I spent scrolling down websites for job openings. Nine times out of ten, searching the internet just ended with me slamming my laptop shut, with a mumbled, "Well, this sucks."

After the days and nights of praying, worrying, and wondering, it hit me. As I sat on the floor fiddling around with a piece of bamboo that I used to practice stick fighting (I love martial arts) and watching an episode of "Halt and Catch Fire," my focus began to hone in as one of the characters was getting in the face of another character and telling him to take his brilliant idea and make something of it. It was a scene of "motivational yelling," if you will.

"*Whoaaaaa,*" I thought as the idea clicked in my head. I could take this time I have to work on starting a martial arts program to help kids with behavioral problems. This idea often floated around in my head. I know the idea itself was not unheard of, but having *my own* program always excited me. I could combine two things I loved – teaching and martial arts. Unfortunately, I had no idea where to start to make this happen. But the way I saw it, if staring at websites all day and applying for jobs wasn't working, why not give it a go? This project wasn't going to be easy, but I had a chance to try. At this point, I realized that I could do *anything*

I wanted. However, what started out as an exciting realization soon became a frustrating reality.

No Confidence? Let's Grab a Drink!

"Hey! Where've you been, brother we missed you last week?" the barista hollered. I looked up as the loud, excited voice carried over all the noise around the café. The barista had a genuine grin on his face as a customer smiled back and reached over the glass case full of pastries. "Welcome back, man! Here's your usual!"

"Thanks, buddy! the customer replied. "Yeah, been out of town. Hey, you have a good one, man! Another day, another dollar!" He grabbed his drink and walked out going about his day.

Many days would pass, and the places I sat to write this book were never short of people walking in and out or chatting at the tiny tables. I always found it funny how some customers would come in their exercise outfits right after a workout and get a big fat frappuccino. I'm not saying I don't go for a cheeseburger after a good exercise, but it's still funny. Other customers wore business suits; some came with notebooks and pens; some came with laptops and smartphones. People wore everything from running shorts, to work boots, to uniforms. I would sit there and sometimes daydream about being one of them. Where would my career hunt take me?

"Maybe one day I'll be walking around town like that lady in a business suit. Or maybe I'll be that mom with a cute toddler on her hip." The toddler screamed, and that daydream quickly ended. I suppose at this point the possibilities were endless, but these mini daydreams were always cut short by reality.

It took me a while to admit to myself that I was more unsure about my future than I wanted to be. Even the high of excitement for my taekwondo program would quickly be brought down by the facts - no money, no resources, no clue. Confession: I spent many days in those coffee shops just trying to "figure things out," and to be completely honest, debating if I really wanted to go through with establishing a program at all. I often wrote in a journal, but the catch was that I would disguise doing so. I would cover the table with notebooks, to make it appear that I was immersed in something important, you know, just in case anyone walking by would care to look at me. Heaven forbid anyone found out I had no clue what I was doing and that I was writing in a journal. How pathetic was that!? Then, one day, those noises around me finally caught my ear, and I woke up, like I had just chugged a big cup of coffee. I'll paint this analogy for you.

Do you recall ever sitting in class at school and slowly feeling anxiety build as the teacher continues with a lesson you don't quite understand? You fall further and further behind with each word the teacher says and you feel like everyone "gets it" but you. You keep a straight face as you frantically scribble notes with the expensive colored pens you bought that up until then, made you feel more organized and studious. Color-coding your notes always works. You scribble away.

"Yup, got it, $x + y = 7$," (scribble scribble) "...divide this by the square root, get 6...Clear as day!" You sit up and proudly look at your notes. *"Hmm, where did 'kinetic energy' come from? Is this even the right notebook? (Blank stare) ... I'll just look at it later and clear it up. In fact, I'll underline 'kinetic energy' in a different color. It must be important."* As you pick a new pen color, you frown and think, *"I am so screwed."* Then you pray to God the teacher doesn't call on you.

Suddenly, out of nowhere you hear a classmate near you mumble, "Where the hell did that number come from?"

Your brain shifts from, *"I'm screwed,"* to *"Oh, thank, God. it's not just me!"* Can I get a Homer Simpson "Woohoo!"? Now I bet that you can fill a room with people, and even the most successful person in the room has felt or will at some point in life share in the feeling of uncertainty, disappointment, or worry. A coffee shop can be that way. Like a bar in the daytime, people come in and out, and some share their stories over a drink.

Have you ever heard the song "Piano Man" by Billy Joel? I believe the words have a way of resonating with many listeners. For those who have never heard it or maybe need to be refreshed on the song, picture a bar full of people with their unique stories to share— their hopes and disappointments and their untouched potential. Ultimately, no matter how unique each character's story is, every story is tied together by a theme—potential successes that will likely never become reality. In my opinion, you know the stories described in this song because of the simple fact that *you are human.* Humans can connect over joy just as much as pain. We can share the feeling of excitement for hopeful dreams. For example, think of the thousands of people cheering on an athlete in the Olympics. But we can also share the feeling of heartbreak in the doubts of ever reaching those dreams. Think of the thousands watching that same athlete come up just short of winning a medal for the second Olympics in a row.

My Moment of Revelation

There are different ways you can approach your dreams (by "dreams" I mean goals). There is living IN the dream, and there is LIVING the dream. Living *in* the dream guarantees that everything goes how you imagine it to go. *Living* the dream involves a bit more work. But hold on, making a dream happen is a *process*, isn't it?

As I sat in coffee shops feeling doubtful about my future, I started to overhear and *listen* to snippets of conversations of people around me. Don't worry, I'm not a creeper. It's like that day in the classroom when you realized you weren't the only one who was confused. When it connects with you, you cannot help but hear a conversation. Let me give you a great example.

One day, two guys, middle-aged, sat to my left. I sat there with my head in my notebooks "looking busy."

"It's been crazy exciting," one of them said. "I've been working on this for years."

"I know, man, I'm excited about it," his friend replied.

"But I gotta be honest," the first guy said. "I hate to just pick up my family and go through all the transition. I don't want to put my kids through that. My wife has been nothing but supportive, but I'm not sure what to do."

I sort of peeked up at them, and his friend just nodded looking really concerned as the budding entrepreneur he sat across from looked down and swirled around the coffee in his paper cup. It was obvious this guy was excited about his new beginning, but just as strong were his feelings of concern, maybe even guilt about the effects on his family.

I learned that coffee shops are not solely a place of craziness at morning rush hour. It is a place to meet with friends, a place to sit alone to relax or to do work. The people who surround you as you sit and sip your drink are more like you than you think. Out of the blue, I realized I was not the only one trying to do something new in my life. Most comforting was the discovery that I was not the only one frustrated with no clue where to begin. I slowly started to see that while I'm on my own trying to figure things out, I wasn't IN it alone. *Everyone* is trying to make "it" happen, whatever "it" is. So, while progress is a goal, progress is a process. We all have our own types of struggles, but we're *all in* it together because, nine times out of ten, *no one ever truly has it together.*

Whenever I looked around, I found comfort in the fact that the man in the boots and a construction hat is in a process in his life just as much as the woman in a business suit or the woman with two kids hanging around her waist and ankles. A friend of mine made a good point. When you roll out of bed to take the necessary steps toward a goal, *anything* you do is progress as long as you're doing something, so just do it. This friend, Thelma, is yet another human just trying to figure out her life. I think that's probably why the two of us get along so well—we're the two kids in the class struggling to get where we want to be.

We all face our realities because we can only run so far from them. We find the process most difficult when our only weapon left in our bag of perseverance is our dreams. Dreams don't pay bills or solve problems but, are dreams powerful. As for me, the strongest tool in my bag of perseverance is God. I've got my dreams tucked in my pocket like anyone else. I just don't quite know what the heck to do with them, or if they're even good for me. At a certain point, it became for me a matter of giving the dreams and troubles to God and letting him point me in the right direction. Then, it's my turn to get to work. So, as I sat there in coffee shops trying to put pieces together, I realized that I was always surrounded by others who weren't perfect. Eventually, *without* shame, I learned to write in my journal without hiding. I finally realized there is no shame in who I am or where I am at *any* time in my life, as long as I'm working toward something good.

How much progress have I made since the moment I started writing this book? Ummmm, let me put it this way—it's all about perspective and knowing what your goal TRULY is. Okay, okaaay, I'll say it. I don't have a martial arts program. I didn't completely fail though. There were two short-lived moments of an after-school martial arts club. One I ran on my own while teaching at a middle school in North Carolina, and a second one I ran with a dear buddy of mine while we taught at a high school in Texas. While neither of the programs looked exactly like what I envisioned, the most important goals that I had were accomplished. The memories and the relationships I built with many of the students were worth every single bit of effort. Both clubs were cut short due to changes in careers. Efforts to keep the dream alive dwindled with these changes. However, I learned that disappointments hold more than just a nice juicy sucker punch. I can't provide objective remedies to struggles we face as people, but keep in mind that no one's life goes exactly according to what they planned, or what they know it can be. Rest assured that everyone is on some kind of journey. If anything, I have learned that there is an abstract art to balancing the motivation of dreams and the driving forces of reality.

2

WHEN THE MUSIC
FADES, GRIT IS GRACE

♪♫

Music for the Mood

"So, what'll it be today?" I ask myself as I give a humongous sigh and start up "Nunny," my red Chevy Cavalier. It is around 5 a.m. and I'm about to head out to work, another day of teaching our youth. It was the same general routine, but I realized that lately there was an addition to the way it started. I pick out a song to get myself motivated to continue this monotonous drag I call work. Think about when you're driving, and a song starts. Sometimes it only takes hearing three notes for you to hit a button and say, "Not today, I can't do that mood." Or maybe instead you hear the notes, smile, and crank it all the way up. Anyway, those crazy kids in my classroom somehow managed to both drive me up the wall *and* make me like them. So I told myself that I'm sticking it out this school year. I didn't move to Texas from North Carolina just to quit.

Back to the music. *"So what'll it be? An uplifting Christian tune to remind myself it's all going to be ok? Nah, I'll just feel worse when I pull up to work and have to stop the song. It's horrible when the encouraging lyrics abruptly end."*

Once that thought crossed my mind, it sparked a bad attitude from within me. My gut told me I was not going to be there (at that job) much longer. I knew it was only a matter of bringing my best each day I had left with the students.

"Way to ruin your morning, Nicole." I immediately started to feel nervous knowing that deep down my disappointment of where I was in life was starting to poke away at my positive morning attitude.

"Ok, new approach," I thought as I tried to focus on the list of songs in my head and push away the bad attitude that was creeping in. *"I'll start my morning ride with a Foo Fighters song so I can scream the anxiety out of my system before I actually get to work."* I started to search for the

songs. *"No, no, no,"* I paused, *"because then I'll just get angry and be angry all day. That's not good. Ok, no Foo Fighters."*

I contemplated a sad song, just to remind me how sad I am. Well, obviously THAT's not a good idea.

"Screw this," I said. I grunted and turned on the car. "My God! I haven't even left home, and I'm already upset," I yelled. I tightened my grip on the steering wheel. "Breathe. Breathe." I felt a "self-pep talk" coming on. You'll find that I do that a lot.

"This is temporary hate of a moment in time, Nicole. God is good," I told myself. "God is good. Just do your best. It is the second half of the school year. Just get to summer. Just get to summer." It took everything in me not to scream and not to cry. So, I kept talking to myself.

"Focus, Nicole. Drive safe." I grunted once more and put the car in reverse. At this point, all the songs I played to motivate myself had gotten old. Irritated, I pressed "shuffle" on my iPod and that would be that.

As I drove down the road, merged onto the highway, and exited back to the regular streets, I didn't pay attention to a single song that played. In fact, I didn't pay attention to anything. Have you ever made it to your destination while driving and when you park you realize that you don't even know how you got there? You just kind of put the car in park and in a confused way go, "Oh. I'm here."

It was still dark out. I pulled up to the school. "Oh, I'm here." I glanced around and saw only the janitor's car in the parking lot. "How the heck is it, that as unmotivated as I am, I still manage to get myself to work early and be productive?" I asked myself. "God's grace, I guess." I shut off the car which also shut off the music. I opened the door and into my ears poured sounds of the cars driving by. Another day, another dollar.

"*I swear that copier in the lounge better not be jammed again,*" I thought as I grabbed my bag, sighed, and headed toward the door.

My Movie Montage

Allow me to shamelessly reveal that I am a sucker for movie montages, especially the motivating ones. You know, those parts in movies where a motivating song blasts in and the character is all of a sudden some badass with an internal drive to overcome. It makes you want to scream a Ric Flair wrestler kind of "Wooooo!" and throw something for no reason other than you're momentarily pumped up? Ok, maybe that's just me, but hey, who *doesn't* like cheering for the victory over the adversity, the cheering on of the good guy?

I'm going to go out on a limb here and assume that every person who reads this, whether you are 15 or 85 years old, has at some point been lost in a daydream. Maybe you received an ESPY award or a Nobel Prize. Or perhaps you and the most amazing person fall in love. If you deny that you have ever been swept away in a daydream, then you need to find either A) a passion, or B) a pulse. Passion drives your life, while a pulse ensures it.

Here's the difficult part about pursuing dreams. It requires problem-solving and persistence. After excitement dies down, you face moments where you realize that playing "Eye of the Tiger" through your headphones while you lift weights won't solve the obstacles you come to face. At times you snap out of the daydream and realize you are standing alone in a puddle of your own failure or heartbreak. Should you one day decide to make a dream a reality (you know, like they do in the movies during the montage) there is that voice that's always in your head. It sets up a competition between your heart and your brain.

"Follow your dreams," it says. "Live your life while you can . . . but don't forget that success requires work and even failure."

But I digress . . . So, what is this movie montage thing of mine? I guess sometimes it is my motivation, and if I'm going to open up to you, then I'll say sometimes it is my four minutes of escape. When something "knocks me down," there is this short-lived moment of anger followed by me telling myself to get up and move on. If my life was ever a movie, this flash of a moment would be where the music kicks in and my blood pumping montage starts.

Why are movie montages able to tug at your emotions the way that they do? While I'm no genius, I would think it's due to the way everything comes together at that moment. Daydreams or music in movies can be tailored to what a person *wants* to hear or happen. Just like I did for my morning drives, people often pick a song to make or match their mood. For example, people pick a song to play while they workout at the gym or go for a run. Picture this. You go to the park to run and sweat out frustration while you crank your jam into the headphones. When your song ends and you're still stuck in the moment, you look up ready to high-five someone. You realize the only people around you are the old lady waiting for her dog to finish pooping and the 6-year-old with a Ninja Turtles helmet rolling by on his scooter. You shrug, soak up whatever adrenaline is left, and just like that, you are back to square one. In movies, actions and music are in sync to make the raw emotion of the moment even more powerful. But what happens when the music fades out in real life?

This, my friends, is where my faith steps in. No matter how much I try to escape facing reality through music or daydreams, eventually the song fades out.

Movie montages only last a minute, and characters' lives change in a couple of hours. I'm sure we all know that life doesn't always happen that way. Eventually we wake up from the dream and must face the world. However, I believe that that chance to wake up is grace, and that grace is also grit.

A Little on My Faith

I know many people have questions about the Catholic faith. Heck, I do, and I was born and raised Catholic. Over time I have come to find that the difference between being a Catholic when you are zero and 30-something years old is that your pursuit of an understanding of your faith and all it encompasses becomes a never-ending journey. The more you learn, the more you realize there is to learn. What's even crazier? You learn to admit that sometimes you are not *meant* to completely understand it. That is the most frustrating and liberating moment.

So why keep practicing my faith? There could be many answers to that question, but I'll explain one of my reasons to continue practicing my faith. The Catholic church has what are called the Seven Sacraments - Baptism, Penance, Eucharist, Confirmation, Holy Orders, Matrimony, and the Anointing of the Sick. I will not go into detail about each of these, as I feel like that would take another book! A general way to explain the Sacraments is that they are simply ways to receive grace from God. To practice and receive these is a beautiful gift and not to be taken lightly. Yes, grace itself can be given by God to anyone at any time. No, grace does not always need to take the form of a formal church ritual. I believe that receiving grace in ways that make you consciously take time to examine your role to others in this world will effectively teach you about who you want to be and how to become a better person. The Sacraments and practices like Eucharistic Adoration, which are offered in the Catholic church, are ways to do just that. So for me, when the "montage music" fades, and when my "workout playlist" no longer gives me the motivating feeling that I *want*, then something is missing. I can't give a name to that "something."

Oddly enough, the Bible defines faith as, "*...the realization of what is hoped for and evidence of things not seen.*"[1] So maybe all along it was my faith that was missing. It's not tangible, and yet, like the feeling of knowing someone cares, it fills a void in your heart. Returning to practices and foundations found in the Sacraments and the simple yet profound practices in church always help me bring my mind and my heart back to a stronger and more hopeful place. It is a place I was introduced to at baptism, before I was even a year old. My friends, I cannot begin to describe the feeling of freedom from worries and regrets that I receive from God. That is something you must do on your own. I would hope you would give it a sincere effort, but keep in mind, it has taken me over 30 years to *barely scratch* the surface of understanding it.

So, let's take the sacrament of Penance. It is also known as reconciliation or going to confession. Have you ever been in a bad situation and all it took were three things to fix it – admitting a mistake, apologizing, and forgiveness? Do you remember how freeing an apology and forgiveness was? Take that to a higher level, and that is often the feeling you get after a genuine confession.

Let's clarify one thing: Confession is not a "fix your problems for good" pill. It doesn't mean you go out, do whatever you want, and just go to confession on Wednesday. It's certainly not designed as an "only use at your convenience" type of act. That's why a person *practices* confession. A child as young as seven or eight begins the practice of confession, and the practice continues until that person dies. Being a Catholic, a Christian, is a lifelong work in progress.

A Halfway Love Affair, a Priest, and a Confession

"Bless me father, for I have sinned. It's been a few months since my last confession." I nervously began my confession as I clasped my hands together. I was bending to get down on the little kneeler, and while I was on the other side of a screen, it was still nerve wracking to see the silhouette of the priest on the other side. As he shifted and leaned over toward the screen to hear me better, I knew that I had to do this. I never thought I'd be going to confession for this.

You see, I had been in the early stages of seeing a man, and in the midst of all the excitement of spending time with someone I liked, I came to learn that this guy had a wife and two kids. He eventually just told me. I'll admit that I'm glad he did, as opposed to my discovering this in alternative ways. But, of course, I was heartbroken. After a day or two of sulking, even though I wasn't "finished" being sad, it hit me…

"Oh, my God. Does this count as me having an affair?!!" I freaked. I talked myself through it. "Ok, I had no clue about his family, so it doesn't count as an affair, right? But I was spending time with him. I mean, I've still got my virginity going for me, right? That's gotta count for something. Something good for me, I mean." I realized that until I went to confession and talked this out, I was only going to be freaking out. Forget being sad about this guy. I was not trying to go to Hell…

It was quiet as the priest waited for me to start talking. I shifted my weight as the scratchy worn-out covering on the kneeler pad started to irritate my knees.

"Um, well," I started. "I had something on my mind, so I thought I'd come in today." I needed to work my way into it. It's not easy to admit a wrong, but as they say, anything worth doing is never easy. I figured priests were probably used to people being nervous. He patiently responded.

"Ok, what is it you would like to tell me today?"

It was now or never.

"Well, I've sort of been seeing a guy, and I found out he has a wife and kids. They are in the middle of a separation, but I had no idea." The silhouette behind the screen suddenly sat up and leaned in closer. I froze and my heart sank.

"Are you still with this man?" he asked me. His tone became stern.

"No. I mean, we were never officially together, just spending more time together than usual. I mean we don't really anymore." I started to freak out.

"But you still see him?"

"Well, kind of. Not dating, but I see him a because of where I work."

"Listen to me," the priest said. "If you truly did not know about his situation, nothing is your fault. But you must get out of this relationship because now you are aware, and it could lead to worse. Not to mention that even if a divorce is completed, this man has a lot to work on in his heart. Who is to say that if he acts this way with his own wife, that he will not do the same to you?"

With my eyes facing down, I quietly replied the only thing that I could think of. "Yes, sir." My heart was broken, but I promised myself I would NEVER let myself be in that situation again. Boy, did I feel like a dummy. There was relief in knowing that the situation wasn't my fault. From what it sounded like, there wasn't an "affair" attached to my situation as long as I got myself out of it and stayed on the right path. I guess I could now focus on healing the heartbreak, knowing I still had a chance with God. I realized that was my hope right there and fixing the relationship with God was more important than the other relationship. No matter how upset I was, it seemed obvious that my fear of God's disappointment ultimately weighed more than anything else.

There was an awkward silence in the tiny room as I knelt there unsure how to feel. I wasn't sure what else to say. At that moment all I wanted to do was go home. I wanted the priest to just wrap it up so I could be on my way. What came out of his mouth to break the silence is forever etched in my mind.

"BURP!"

He burped. He burped *loudly*. I'm pretty sure it came from pretty deep down, and the people waiting in line outside heard it.

I lifted my widened eyes up from bowing down and pressed my lips together as hard as possible trying not to laugh.

"I'm sorry, excuse me," he said. His silhouette now leaned back.

Naturally, the laughter I was holding on the other side of my pressed lips came spewing out of my nose instead. I quickly tried to pull myself together.

Most awkward confession. Ever.

You know, my mom always told me that God has a sense of humor. I don't know if that was proof of it, but if it was, God has the worst timing. Or maybe the best timing. Did you ever get into an argument with a friend, and it's followed by that awkward moment of tension in silence? Then one of you says a smart-ass remark and regardless of your effort to stay upset, all you can do is try not to laugh. That is what that moment in confession felt like. At some point, you know the healing must begin, but you know you are still loved. So, I got myself back on track, and I moved on. I had to eventually walk out of church and as the day went on and the tension of confession faded away, a feeling of freedom in my mind and heart started to take over. I knew there would still days I would be sad or mad, but I knew that the hardest part was over. Now I just had to do my best to live better.

"Go In Peace..."

There is this Catholic church in Houston, Texas, that like many other churches is simply embedded into the community around it. Neighborhoods surround about three quarters of it, and along the busier street is a soccer complex, a gas station, and a tiny building that used to be a burger place. Within that church, people gather every single day of the week to pray and take part in mass. Like many churches, the people are involved in the community, whether working with the local food bank, providing resources for people in search of work, or holding everyone's favorite event – the fish fry.

I attended this church for nearly four years before moving back to North Carolina. In the same way a movie montage can whisk you away and momentarily recharge your battery of motivation, going to church does this for me. For a moment in time whether I am listening to the priest or the music on Sunday, or kneeling in front of the Blessed Sacrament in the middle of the week, my mind is redirected to something bigger than myself or my problems.

Here's the kicker – just like how the music and inspiration slowly fades away in a movie, so too does that feeling in church. After an hour or so, the music, the readings, communion, are over and I have to place myself outside of the church walls to face everything in the world that I had *just* brought to God to take care of.

Every disappointment and frustration I gave up to God is still waiting for me when I go home. The bill I have to pay still needs to be paid. That difficult relationship with a friend must still be dealt with. The stressful and monotonous tasks I am so tired of doing must still be done. I mean, did God *really* just solve or eliminate all my problems while I was in church? Well, no. It doesn't work that way. A good life requires work.

One Sunday in Houston, one of the priests was talking to the congregation. He pointed to the ceiling where there is a huge light fixture above the altar. It is solid with only several openings that held light bulbs. Having once studied to become an architect, I tried to grasp any type of design concept. I had always thought it looked like an arrow, but I never thought anything else of it.

"You see that big arrow above our altar?" said the priest. Everyone looked up. "You know what that is? That is a reminder to each of us. It reminds us that the world is out there, and that is the direction God is pointing you to go." Sure enough, that arrow that is like a roof over the crucifix and the altar points right to the doors of the church. To the *outside*. I sat there, and that message hit home. If the architect did that on purpose, he or she is pretty darn good.

I realized that I rely on going to church each week to "restore" myself from whatever mess I got into that previous week. It's like I add to this box of problems all week and bring it into church every Sunday. Like a puppy proudly wagging its tail and dropping a dead animal at its owner's feet, I bring my box of problems each Sunday and say, "Here you go God!" I sit in church and slowly calm my heart down. By the end of church, I HATE leaving because it means I have to face everything I don't want to face. By the following week I've managed to refill my box of problems, often times the exact same ones I had the week before. I come to God to get myself right; I try my best to remember to say thank you, I ask for forgiveness, and I ask for help. Just like the music fades out in a movie or through my headphones, time in church comes to an end and I need to get out and get back to work. I have to *work*. At the end of every mass, the priest gives a simple instruction.

"Go in peace to love and to serve the Lord."

And we reply, "Thanks be to God."

I *should* be thankful. Despite all the problems I bring him, God continues to bless me and God believes in me enough to *actually* send me back out into the world.

So, I decided from then on to be sure to leave my worries in church, and take courage with me when I step out the doors to pick up where I left off, no matter how ugly it looks or what other people may think. You know how people tell you to hurry up? That whole "I got people to see, things to do" type deal? Well, at some point God will send you out in a hurry too, and sometimes it feels like a swift kick in the butt. Sometimes, it breaks your heart and makes no sense.

"You can't get too comfortable!" God says. "I've got people for you to see and things for you to do! I need your help. So go on. I'm looking out for you, I know what I'm doing. Don't worry." As Jesus instructed his disciples before sending them out into the world, *"Whoever will not receive you or listen to your words – go outside that house or town and shake the dust from your feet."*[2] Even when the music fades, God's grace is my grit. If you've got grit, you don't simply quit.

3

BLAST ON

♪♪

"Ok, you can go now," he said as he nodded toward
the door. I walked out of his office for the last time,
leaving the rickety wooden chair in the same place it
always was. Once I walked out of his office, I started
shaking. I don't even recall what I was thinking or feeling
for the next few minutes. All I remember feeling was
that it was done. I took a deep breath and looked up.

"Thank you, God," I whispered. "It's over."

One of the hardest walks I ever took led me out of
a place I loved so dearly. It was a place where I learned

so much, where I felt needed, where I belonged. To this day, I can easily replay that difficult afternoon. I remember throwing my bag over my shoulder and walking toward the door feeling angry, sad, and upset. While my mind battled confusion, I walked past familiar sounds, sights, and smells. There was a desire to take one last look around, but I didn't need to. I knew where every chair, poster, and banner was placed, and even what was in every closet. While I didn't want to leave that place, I wanted to get out of there as fast as possible.

As I walked toward the door to leave, a few people were still standing around chatting, the people who knew what was going on and understood why I would never be back. It was dead silent as I walked by, and I seemed to almost feel their concerned stares. It was as if they were hugging me without hugging me. I wanted more than anything to say goodbye, but I knew the only way to get out without crying was to look down and keep walking. So that's what I did.

Some people want to be tough, whether it's a matter of pride or that's just who they are. Me? I like to think I am tough, but the truth is that I hate confrontation. I admit that I am very passive-aggressive. Growing up, I irritated my mom just like every other kid, but it wasn't how I dressed or because I got into trouble at school. It was allowing myself to be pushed around. It was rare that anyone ever physically bullied me. What happened more often was that people would take advantage of how I tended to let a lot of things go. Sometimes I was a little too nice. I was generally happy, and I got along with kids from all walks of life. I never got into fights or arguments. I found that being a little more laid back and just being friendly paid off in many ways. Avoiding trouble was easy, and I often think it was because bullies were bored with me. I could've been an easy target—always the smallest person, sometimes a little on the nerdy side. I found that people responded well to a "laid back" personality. It's who I am, and I was content. Unfortunately, a time finally came where "shaking" the bad feeling and just letting something go didn't work. For once in my life, I had to *face* something and someone. To make it worse, that someone was a person I had admired.

A Rude Awakening

I will not exaggerate anything I am going to describe because that is not necessary. I don't doubt that someone has dealt with the same thing, and unfortunately some deal with worse. Simply take it for what it is. I am writing on this topic to demonstrate the power of resilience when paired with faith and to demonstrate the importance self-respect when you want to move on in life.

I will begin by telling you that my initial reaction was shock. What started out as a usual lunch led to an awkward conversation and John's request to see a picture of me in a bathing suit. I tried to quickly find a way to shift the conversation to something else while also trying to process in my mind if the current conversation was a "red flag." Well, of course it was a red flag. It's easy to see *now*, and it's easy to see if you're on the outside looking in. As I tried to process things, I realized that John's hands were making their way up my leg, well above my knees. I froze in place. My heart started to beat faster and my stomach was in my throat as I realized I did NOT want to be in this situation. I wanted him to leave.

"What the hell is happening? No way," was all I could think. In the several seconds that felt like ages, his hands wandered around my arms and under my shirt. The inside of me screamed for him to stop, but all I could do was awkwardly step to the side and walk toward the table. I was just trying to get away. I couldn't come up with words or actions. Who knew your mind could be racing but go completely blank at the same time?

"I'll go now," he said as he walked toward me. I started to worry because walking *toward* me meant walking *away* from the door.

"Oh God, please make him go away NOW," screamed in my mind.

"Ok, come on, just give me a hug," he said.

"Uhhh, ha," was all I could get out. He approached me and began to wrap his arms around me tight. I twisted myself sideways to try to avoid the hug and avoid any acknowledgement of touching in any way.

"What? You don't like it when I hug you?" he laughed as he then let go and stepped back. His slight change in tone freaked me out. I panicked knowing now would not be a good time to piss him off. I simply wanted out of the situation.

"No, not really. I don't," I stated.

"Oh," he said, "I thought you did. Well, come on ok, just one hug." He approached me again, and I stepped and turned to the side once again. He took the hint, stared for a moment looking a little irritated. Then he walked out. I never realized until then how incredibly long a couple minutes could feel.

The second he walked out, I locked the door right behind him and set my security alarm. I stood with my mouth open and my thoughts shifted from, *"What is happening?"* to *"Did that just happen . . . to me?"* I slowly walked to my dining table, and suddenly started to briskly clean by throwing away EVERYTHING he touched, I didn't care. Throw that shit away. Dishes and silverware went straight to the garbage. Who cares if they were good dishes? I never wanted to touch them again.

Running them through the dishwasher numerous times wouldn't do away with the kind of dirty I was feeling. In a panic, I wiped down the table and chairs, first with Pledge, then with Lysol, and a third time just spraying with Lysol. I then proceeded to clean the couch, the sink faucet, and the doorknob . . . clean, clean, clean. I felt so dirty! Then I just put all the cleaning supplies down and slowly sat down, mouth hanging open.

"No. No way," kept repeating in my brain. But deep down I thought I should be honest. Something did happen. At that point, a cycle of hurt, confusion, and anger grew inside of me.

About a week after the incident, I realized that I could not be passive-aggressive this time. It took a lot of guts, but I marched right up to John and directly said that I did not appreciate what happened and I never want it to happen again. He said ok. It took me about another week to realize that I didn't feel any better. I slowly started to admit that perhaps I was in denial, and this was in fact a REAL problem - the inappropriate touching and the way it mentally impacted me. When I was anywhere near John, I cringed at his voice alone. When I heard his footsteps getting closer, I chose to go a different direction. I didn't want to see him, hear him, or be near him, even if we were surrounded by other people. I remember one day, as I waited for him to leave, I stood around the corner of a wall just listening for when he walked out. Standing there, I felt a wave of sadness as I slowly admitted to myself how wrong this was, how much I didn't like hiding or the way that I felt. I began to realize that I couldn't let myself be in an environment that would only fill me with anxiety and toy with whatever was left of my self-confidence and steady mind. NO one should allow that for themselves. What made me worry even more, was that as hard as I tried to find it, for once in my life there was no voice in my head to help me toughen up.

I waited anxiously for, "You got this, Nicole, stick it out. You're tough."

Nope, I couldn't hear that voice. Instead it sounded more like, "I don't like this."

As much as I tried to ignore and suppress it, that tiny voice only became louder. It was difficult to admit to myself that I couldn't handle the amount of discomfort I was in. Even more difficult was admitting that I may never get over anything if I don't *do* anything. To begin with, getting out of there soon was a *must*. Period.

The next few days consisted of praying for strength and guidance. I constantly rehearsed in my head what I would say to John. Then, it was time to finally approach him. As I tried to pep talk myself into moving my feet toward his office, I couldn't tell if I wanted to throw up, cry, or both. My mom once told me that if you always do right, then God is always on your side and there is no need to worry. My problem is that I hate two things: confrontation and when people are mean – when they just consciously or intentionally do wrong. I don't care to fight with anyone about it, but I can get a little teary-eyed. While some people may see that as a weakness, I choose to see it as a gift. If anything, becoming upset with wrongdoing lets me know that my conscience still works. I'm grateful for that.

I finally, took a deep breath and I began walking toward John's office door. I knocked and poked my head in.

"Excuse me," I felt my voice shake, and my heart raced. I continued, "Can I talk to you for a minute?"

"Sure," he said. "Come on in, sit down."

I started to close the door but left a small crack for my own comfort. Looking up, I saw he looked a little surprised that I closed the door that far. He usually kept it open, you know, an "open door policy."

"Maybe he'll take me seriously now," I thought.

I sat down at the table in his office. That familiar wooden chair that I once felt so privileged to sit in while he would teach me about the ins and outs of the business, the same chair I would sit in when he gave me advice about life, it was now just a creaky old chair.

"God help me," I thought as I sat down, *"I can do all things with you. Let's do it."*

That day, a different kind of courage stirred in me. I'll give credit to the Holy Spirit and my mom's advice. For the one of the hardest confrontations in my life, I did not back down from any response thrown at me. John's responses to anything I said not only fueled my fire but also exposed more of him as a person. Amazingly enough, I learned more about him in those - what seemed like a zillion minutes than in the several years I'd been around him. The night before, I rehearsed a million times a ridiculous speech, but of course instead of the Oscar-winning drama-filled climactic scene I had played out in my head, it came out more straightforward.

"I didn't appreciate what happened. Don't ever do it again," I blurted.

"*SHIT!* I thought to myself as my heart raced. *"Didn't I already say that the other day? I'm pretty sure I had rehearsed more than that last night. It was like a 15-minute speech! Oh God! What was I gonna say again?!"* For a moment my fear left because I was too busy trying to remember what to say. I wanted to hold up my hand and restart. You know, kind of like:

"Hold on a second, man I know I had something else to say. Give me a minute."

"Hmmm," I thought, *"maybe I can walk out, and come back in. No, that's ridiculous. Just stay steady now."* Then John responded.

"Ok. I'm sorry. I won't."

In my mind, that conversation seemed too short and too easy. I felt like he didn't quite get what I was saying. So, I opened my mouth again.

"No, I *really* don't want anything like that to happen again. I've decided to leave." Now, I didn't expect tears from him, but maybe some kind of reaction would've been nice. He stood up. Not the reaction I was hoping for. He paused.

"Ok, I will let you go," he said.

I stood there and in my mind I saw my right eyebrow raise up really high. I had to pause and think through in my head, *"I'm sorry. Did this fool just say he'll 'LET me go?'"* I'm pretty sure at that point I had no problem leaving that place, and whatever speck of respect I had left for him was hanging on by a thread.

"Did you tell anyone else?" he continued. "Not about leaving, but about what happened?" That question pretty much cut that last thread.

"Yes, I did." I stood there in disbelief that John's greatest concern was who knew what happened as opposed to what actually happened or that I was leaving. The truth is, I had told three others because I wanted them to be aware, and to be safe.

"Who else knows?" John asked. He started to walk around his desk. I stood my ground.

"It doesn't matter who knows, and I won't tell you," I replied. "I just wanted to let you know that I will be leaving."

John proceeded, "Ok, but if anyone asks why you're leaving, just tell them that you have too many obligations, you're too busy with school or work."

You want to add insult to injury? Up until then, John was a mentor of sorts to me. When a mentor does something so horrible and then asks you lie about it, that will definitely challenge your perception of him or her.

"Sir," I told him as he walked toward me. He stopped between the side of his desk and a bookcase. "I do not lie to people. I have no interest in telling details, but I will not lie if they ask me anything."

He slowly sat back down, just looking at me. I finally woke up to the fact that some people honestly put themselves and their reputation first. Everything John once appeared to be – highly respectable, a role model - flew out the window. Was everything I believed about him a lie? Maybe, maybe not. I wanted very much to leave room for a benefit of the doubt. Somehow, deep down, I felt sorry for him. While I was hit hard that day by a huge dose of who John really was, I could not help but want to hang on to whatever bit of a good heart I tried to believe was in him. I truly believe everyone has at least little bit in them, no matter how small. It just doesn't make sense not to believe it. A priest once told me that people lie because they are afraid. If John wanted to lie, he must have been scared.

I told him that I forgave him, and I don't know what he thought of that. Forgiving didn't mean that it would ever be the same, but I knew I had to tell him. So, I did. Simple as that. As I stood there in front of John fueled by every emotion under the sun, and more confident in my decision to leave, I made my last attempt to ensure that I walked away not necessarily with the last word of the conversation, but more importantly, that I walked away with no regrets. I just looked straight in his eyes across the desk, sat up straight, and spoke firmly.

"I forgive you, you know."

There was no change to his tone of voice, no tears in his eyes. There was no change in my tone of voice, no tears in my eyes. He just stared at me, and I stared right back.

Silence.

"Ok, you can go now," he finally replied.

To be honest, I just wanted to leave with both of us in peace. Neither of us had to end the conversation liking the other, but I wanted as much bitterness out of my system as possible. I figured that as a Christian, it's what I was supposed to do. Forgive. Maybe that mindset of "because I'm supposed to," is wrong. Look, I ain't perfect, but I figured I've got to start somewhere.

Perhaps if I just started by saying the words "I forgive you," I would eventually feel a kind of peace. Over time, it certainly helped, and even if my heart was still filled with confusion for a long while, there was always a sense of peace and comfort knowing that my last words to him were that I forgave him. I may have left hurt, but I think that is better than leaving bitter.

Looking back now, I realize that the little office that I once felt so privileged to be a part of, that little office that played a big role for a moment of my life, is *just* a little office. The world beyond John's door only became bigger and full of more opportunity once I gathered the courage to step outside of what I thought was going to be my future.

That is God's grace. "Grace" seems to carry a sort of soft and positive connotation. However, it takes many forms, including let downs and an end to wonderful things. I went after my own dreams, and God made sure I stayed out of that door. On the flip side, God opened up the world for me. Walking out that door set me free to explore the world I never would have bothered to see. Grace is grit.

Let the Healing (at Least) Begin...

A couple of weeks after the incident, I found myself sitting in the little waiting room of a clinic reading a kid's *Highlights* magazine. Seeing any kind of counselor never really crossed my mind. I was upset, but I didn't feel like it hindered my well-being or functioning. A couple of friends kept mentioning that it is always an option if needed. Being allowed three free counseling sessions through my job at the time, I figured why not try at least once?

I sat in the waiting room occupying myself with the *Highlights* magazine searching for the hidden ice cream cones on the activity page. I found the search way more entertaining than the *Glamour* or business magazines scattered on the end tables. As my eyes casually scanned the page of the magazine, my mind spent more time wondering what this counseling session would be like. Would I be lying on some big couch across from the counselor? Would the counselor be male or female? I honestly felt kind of silly. Truthfully, I felt like all I needed was time to just let things pass and I'd be back on track. I have nothing against seeing a counselor. Different people have different ways of coping, and if a counselor is what you need, I'm happy the option is there. But did I need it?

Honestly, I don't remember much of the session at all. It wasn't bad, but it wasn't beneficial either. Other than the counselor asking me a bunch of questions on life events, medical history, things like that, I just sat there feeling kind of weird. There was no couch, but instead a huge armchair. The room had dark curtains and a lava lamp. The counselor sat in a big armchair with her clipboard. That made me paranoid as I kept wondering what she was writing. I appreciated what she did, but truthfully, I left the place feeling more confident in my ability to just get through things on my own, perhaps with the support of my friends.

As you'll find out in a future chapter, I "accidentally" discovered that a counselor was exactly what I needed. Talking was all it took to realize how many thoughts and feelings I suppressed for several years and talking was all it took to get it out of my system. What a relief! Who knew?

A Matter of Respect

Vulnerabilities and self-doubt. Like a lot women, I would love to meet that "Prince Charming." I am not going to hide the fact that I am at the lowest level of flirting expertise, but I've come to accept that and have grown to love who I am more and more. On the plus side, experiences like my confession with the burping priest and with John have helped me put some space between myself and the "gotta be married by age 27" bandwagon. I'll be happy to meet a wonderful man, but searching or chasing after someone is not going to be my source of happiness. Learning to accept and respect who you are and where you are in life is a pretty big step to happiness, whether you are single or not.

I cannot tell you that I never thought everything that happened with John was my fault. The thing is, I have a quiet confidence, and while I knew it wasn't my fault, the thought used to creep in every now and then. Friends would tell me that I was not at fault for what John did, but whenever I wallowed in my puddle of "I wish nothing ever happened," my mind easily started to throw all kinds of questions around.

"Why didn't I see it coming? Am I that dumb? I'm pretty sure I never flirted with John, and I couldn't have provoked anything."

What made it worse was that whenever I went through things in my head, all the "red flags," popped up like a mole in a Whack-a-Mole game.

"How could I have been so stupid!?" I would ask myself in frustration.

To top it all off, I started to wonder that if some wonderful man ever came around in my life and learned of what happened, would I suddenly look like trash?

"Girl, you are *not* trash," I would tell myself. I know this, and I *believe* it. The problem was, would everyone else believe it?

Here are two messages for males and females alike. It is simple: you are awesome, and treat everyone with respect, including yourself. Now there is a brilliant concept. It starts with the simple things. For example, just because someone has gigantic muscles doesn't mean you shouldn't offer to help him or her carry something when their hands are full. At least hold the door. On the receiving end, if someone sincerely offers to help you, try not to take offense. So often people preach about being kind…so if someone is *actually* trying to do that, don't smash their willingness. Be thankful people in this world are trying. Spread the positivity and just say thank you. No harm done, no time wasted, and hopefully you have kept the cycle of kindness moving. If they say "screw you," instead, well, just move on.

Now, let's not forget the most important person to respect – YOURSELF. The respect you show yourself will ultimately reflect in the way you allow others to treat you. I'm pretty sure that's a recurring quote, so I'm not taking credit for it. I just thought I'd mention the concept.

I realized a lot of things in the few months following the incident with John. However, one that stands out is go with your gut. One night, I was finding some consolation in Steven, a friend who also knew John. Steven told me that what happened with John was not my fault.

"You trusted that man," he told me. "Up until this mess, you had good reason to trust him. Heck, I trusted him. Now, even I don't know if I do, and that upsets me." Steven's words were starting to make me see the whole situation in a new light.

"Look," he continued. "John took advantage of your *trust*, not your stupidity."

"HEY!" I shouted laughing, "what stupidity?" He laughed.

"I just mean that he was good, and by good, I mean good at being bad." Steven was right. In my state of shock and confusion with John, I just froze. In that moment, I didn't know what to do even though I knew what I needed to do.

When watching a movie, it's really easy to roll your eyes and just scream at that "dumb girl" getting attacked or chased on the screen.

"Really!?" you want to shout at the actress. "Kick him in the nuts! Oh, my God, run you idiot…Poke him in the eyes! For goodness sake, stab his ass! You grabbed a knife so use it! Ugh, really?! Yeah, run up the stairs instead of out the door genius." In your own frustration with the character, you throw up your arms and reach for another handful of popcorn.

I learned that in real life, if a person that you have trusted for a long time catches you off guard (I mean mentally, not physically) it *can* be hard to react. I heard somewhere that, often, acts of things like sexual harassment or assault are committed by a relative or someone that the victim knows. People are often too scared or too busy trying to make sense of what's happening before they can react. I was in no way attracted to John, so it was a no brainer that I did not want what was happening. But, I froze. I would like to think that now I would have no problem punching someone square in the face the minute I felt something wasn't right. I learned my lesson. Unfortunately, it took a rude awakening to make that "click" in my brain. So, ladies and men, if your gut knows something is going down a path that makes you uncomfortable, get out of the situation before it goes too far. And if it's hard to do *please* find someone you can trust to help you. If someone ends up hating you for standing up for yourself, then obviously that idiot ain't worth your time and effort. SELF-respect comes first. Know that you are worth just as much as anyone else in this world. Don't be afraid to protect that.

Go Ahead, Burn That Bridge

Practicing martial arts has always been something that I enjoy, and it has helped me both physically and mentally. One time, I was practicing board breaking for a demonstration. A group of us were trying out different board breaks, and this particular time I was training to do a flying side-kick jumping over three people. At this point, I was still getting a feel for it and practicing by jumping over stacks of kicking pads. Jump after jump,

I kept either rocking or knocking off the top pad at the end of the row. Seeing my frustration, my instructor walked over to me and looked me square in the face.

"Fly," he said. He just looked very sternly into my eyes.

"What?" I said. I got what he was saying. Fluffy inspirational words were great, but at this point I was just frustrated, so at first, "fly" didn't do a thing to help me. I just stared at him, completely clueless.

"Fly," he said. His tone shifted to less stern. But he just stared right at me. "You have everything you need to do the kick. You have speed, you can jump, you have the right timing, you have power. You will easily break the board. Stop trying to jump forward. Jump UP. Fly. Your momentum will carry you. *Just fly*." Then he walked away. From then on I cleared every jump without a single problem.

* * *

They say "burning bridges" is bad, but I think that if burning the bridge sets you free, it's ok. The way I think about it is that if I can fly, I don't need a bridge anyway. In life, there are many lessons in strength and humility and how to trust and take care of yourself. Like when doing a flying side kick, I have everything I need to get over obstacles. It is a matter of trusting myself and letting it carry me. Even more important, I must take care of myself in order to get past obstacles. Sometimes that means burning a bridge. It might mean letting go of things, like a bad experience, a bad relationship, or anything that weighs you down. It might also include letting go of something you love so that you can move on. I learned that at times, allowing your heart to break is the first step in discovering that it is in fact the correct time to move forward. I came across this quote not too long after the incident with John. Sorry, I can't recall where I saw it, but it sure did stick in my mind:

"Sometimes you feel bad or hurt, not because you did something wrong, but because you did what was right."

I chose to tell my story about John because I feel like the lessons learned were worth sharing. I feel like my experience might be helpful to someone. Pull from it what you will – the importance of self-respect, importance of not letting the world get you down, lessons about forgiveness, about never completely healing but never letting it stop you, about will power, about betrayal, and the list goes on. I've learned that my story also goes on. The power of prayer and trusting what God wants for you is what has always kept me going. Part of growing up is realizing that chasing what you want can sometimes be the wrong goal to chase.

Ladies and men who have ever faced anything similar to my experience with John, I think it's safe to say that most—if not all of us—have each other's backs.

You are not alone. You are awesome. It is not about whose story is more horrific or unfortunate because let's face it, in our own personal minds, our story is as bad as it gets. The point is we are in it together. Be who you are and treat yourself and others with respect and kindness. The world really would be a lot better off.

Here is my concluding point: Sometimes, there is no fluff or "movie montages" to play out. Sometimes life boils down to just yucky things and getting through them. I was once told by someone that fear is your worst enemy. He always told me that even if you are afraid, you can't be afraid the second you make the decision to take action. The irony? That someone was John. But he is right. Don't let fear stop you.

I made the decision to learn and move on because if I didn't, the time I would have wasted would have been only my own fault. And I sure as hell ain't afraid to move on. Since we have been tying in martial arts, I'll leave you with one of my favorite Bruce Lee quotes:

"Go bravely on, my friend, because each experience teaches us a lesson. Keep blasting because life is such that sometimes it is nice and sometimes it is not." [1]

4

I Heard Black Sheep Sing Miley Cyrus

♪♫

It all began with my style—or lack thereof. Over time it became apparent that the paths that I chose and the way in which I did things were often stumbled upon. For whatever reason, I often stray from the "normal" path. But, it's ok.

Almost Cool

Who knew standing at a bus stop in middle school would have such a profound impact on keeping a person motivated in adulthood? Like many people, middle school presented me with challenges and awkward moments, but I made it through by the grace of God. In the process, I learned quite a bit about myself.

I started middle school within a couple weeks of moving back to the U.S. from Germany. With that move came a lot of adjusting. I was used to changing schools since my dad was in the military. I was generally shy as a kid. I never had trouble getting along with people, but it took a while to make friends and find other kids I was comfortable being around. Middle school was my first time in a school that was not on a military base, and even worse, my first time having to ride a school bus. I still cringe at the thought and missed walking to school. A bus is great if you are a social butterfly, but a nightmare if you are an introvert.

Typical of life in middle school, there were moments where fitting in was all of a sudden life or death. Efforts to fit in only reminded me that I was a little bit different. Eventually I also realized I didn't "stray too far" from others. Nevertheless, many days felt like a test of my level of coolness.

I remember that someone on the bus would always have a copy of the *Eastbay Catalog* and people would gather around it shouting about which shoes they thought were "da bomb," in other words, cool. Knowing good and well I would never own a pair of the latest Fila or Nike

Air shoes (yes, this was the '90s) I would still squeeze my tiny self through people to take a peek and at the very least attempt to be some part of the conversation. Glancing at the pages of the catalog I found that while I thought some shoes were kind of cool, there were other styles that caused me to struggle to keep my face from showing what I really thought, *"Eeew."*

One time, a boy named Ed turned to me and asked, "Hey Nicole, which of these two shoes do you like better?"

I went straight into panic mode, surprised anyone asked my opinion. I didn't even know people knew I was there. I instantly felt a ton of pressure to choose "correctly." I quickly pointed to a picture and waited for Ed to respond. I felt like I was waiting for the verdict at my own trial. His response?

"Oh, ok, your taste is pretty good," he said.

I just kind of stared. I thought, *"Uuuhh, thanks?"* Part of me was relieved that I "passed the test," while another part of me wanted to just slap him. My "taste is *pretty* good?" But when I thought about it, I guess "pretty good taste," was better than being made fun of for my taste. I just shrugged and decided to take it as a compliment.

One time, I wore one of my favorite green shirts to school. I remember there was a boy I had a crush on standing next to me waiting to get into the classroom. He looked at me with his adorable, freckled face and smiled.

"Hey, I like your shirt," he said.

I almost pissed on myself, but I played it cool.

"Oh, thanks," I replied.

"Where'd you get it, looks like American Eagle or something?" he asked as all of us slowly herded into the classroom.

In my attempt to just keep the conversation flowing, I just gave the honest answer, "Oh it's from the PX."

"Dude," I thought, *"everyone better be listening to this conversation because this guy is cute, and apparently I have a nice shirt."*

He stared for a second and said, "Oh," then just proceeded into the room.

"Dude," I thought, *"I hope NO ONE heard that conversation."*

So much for that moment of awesomeness. He either had no clue what store that was or he was not impressed. "PX" is short for the Post Exchange. It is a retail store I grew up with living on Army bases. I always thought it was a decent store. Oh well.

To be honest, I was never into a lot of fashion. I was content with a pair of jeans, a t-shirt, and tennis shoes.

They were comfortable, so why not? In truth, I liked looking at how other girls dressed and I "studied styles" carefully, but I didn't care enough to follow styles or stress myself out trying to afford it. I was pretty accepting of myself being hopeless in that department. However, like anyone else that age, of course I wanted to fit in. Let's just say my choice of favorite sport, favorite clothes, or favorite TV shows, didn't exactly match any of the cool kids' preferences. While most kids watched TRL on MTV, I watched *Xena, Warrior Princess*. In the medium sized military town of Fayetteville, North Carolina, football, basketball, and the marching band were usually the more popular extra-curricular activities. I liked those things too, they just weren't my top choices. So, I generally kept my main interests to myself. Despite the ever-present peer pressure, I believe that ultimately, I embraced my uniqueness. Up until college, I was a fairly quiet person. I was good at a lot of things, but I had no problem *not* being the center of attention. Occasionally I was forced into it, but I guess that's a good thing. If anything, awkward and/or embarrassing moments make for great future stories that can become both inspiring and humorous.

It'll Pay Off

One cool fall morning, I was standing at the bus stop with the usual group of kids. We stood around the yellow fire hydrant at the corner chatting about whatever you chatted about in middle school - some episode on TV, who had a crush on who, or the latest cool shoes. The general conversation that fall morning was no different than any other, and honestly, I can't even remember any of it. I can't remember any of it except for the one tiny statement someone made to me… "Don't worry, it'll pay off someday."

Now, whatever the topic of conversation was, I can clearly recall that as usual, I started to become more and more detached from the conversation. I stood there with my violin case holding it so that it stood on its end. Truthfully, I sometimes felt out of place because I got good grades and I *liked* school. In other words, I often felt like a nerd. Carrying that violin did not help. I mean, an Asian who likes school and plays the violin. Really?

Was it weird that I felt a little out of place, a "black sheep" of sorts, whether I "fulfilled" the Asian stereotype or wanted to step completely out of the box? When you are unsure about who you are, you figure out how to make who you are convenient. For example, being Asian it is ok to like school. The problem comes when you realize that some people will not take you seriously when you are interested in something you are not "supposed to be" interested in, or you are *not* interested in something you are "supposed to be" interested in. For me, it was things like enjoying and playing sports. When it came to music, I initially wanted to play percussion in the band. However, the class filled up before I could register, and all that was open was the orchestra. Orchestra ended up being one of, if not my all-time favorite class, and while I still find a happy place playing drums, I don't regret picking up the violin. I think it is a beautiful instrument. But, back to the bus stop…

As I stood there and listened to the other kids talk, I became a little more uncomfortable. When that happened, I would always pretend to tinker with my violin case and try to look like I wasn't paying attention to the conversation. I'd spin it around on its end, flip the little clasps, or I would play with the little stuffed pink bunny that my mom gave me that I had attached to the case handle. As I tinkered away listening to the other kids, I got nervous. It seemed like the conversation was steering closer and closer to me getting dragged into it. Soon enough someone was going to ask me about my opinion on something or worse, someone would say something hurtful. Hey, at least according to Ed my taste in shoes was ok. Do you have any idea how tight I clung to that "compliment" from Ed to reassure myself that I was not a loser? I just kept staring down at my violin case while I frantically tried to figure out how to get myself out of the situation before—God forbid—my precious 12-year-old feelings were hurt. So, what did I do? When the next moment of silence in the conversation presented itself, I simply blurted out the first defensive line I could come up with. If I talked first, I wouldn't suffer the discomfort of being forced to talk.

"Well, I've always been different so . . . yeah." I didn't *shout* it out defensively, I really just kind of blurted it out of nowhere in hopes of nipping that conversation in the bud. *"Eat that,"* I thought.

Aaaannnd, in my mind crickets chirped. Without looking up, I knew all eyes were on me. So much for drawing attention *away* from me.

For a split second, I thought I had succeeded at keeping attention away from me. Then I realized I did the complete opposite. *"Oh shit,"* I sighed and looked down. The little pink bunny was more pleasant to focus on anyway. Along with embarrassment, that familiar panic mode started to creep in. I felt my face get hot, and I think the imaginary crickets even stopped chirping to stare at me. But the first words to break the silence threw me off completely.

"Don't worry, it'll pay off someday," I heard a familiar voice say. It was Chrissy.

"Is that a compliment, or are you being sarcastic?" I grappled with the statement, but just like with Ed, I shrugged and decided it was a compliment. Only this time, I felt like it actually *could* be a compliment. Those words stick with me to this day. Thanks, Chrissy. I think you are right, being different has paid off, and I feel

like there is still a lot more for me to venture into in this life. When I start to worry that I'm not quite well-established in a career, Chrissy's words reassure me that not following the world's expectations isn't necessarily a bad thing.

Class Is in Session

Middle school wasn't completely miserable. I eventually figured out which kids I liked to be around. An important lesson was that not all popular kids are jerks...and not all nerds are friendly. You must get to know a *person*, not their reputation. Another great thing was that I was finally old enough to play school sports. And, through orchestra class, I learned that I liked to play music. While I wasn't superb at playing, I certainly wasn't bad either. Along with how to solve algebraic equations, a few history facts, and learning how uncool my Trapper Keeper was, I picked up three pretty important lessons in middle school.

Lesson 1: Slow is not dumb.

Quite often I approach and do things in a very different way. You can call it "methodical," or "cautious," or whatever you want. Whenever I wanted to participate in anything (academic, athletic, artistic, or social) and I saw or listened to other kids participating, I realized I didn't really think like any of them, or nearly as fast as they did. I knew I wasn't slow, seeing as how I always did well in school. For some reason, I just didn't process information as quickly as others, at least not at the moment the information was given to me. It always took me just a second longer to "catch on." As discouraging as that was, I started to feel like God put way deep within me a quiet faith and confidence in myself and my abilities. He then paired it nicely with probably the most cowardly looking courage ever. But I learned that for whatever reason, I will always put myself out there and try my best in any situation.

Lesson 2: Your self-consciousness is actually an investigation into who you are, and a painful process of converting your "flaws" into what you should learn to love about yourself.

I wasn't going to grow any taller. I will always have my stalky legs and short fingers. However, I have grown (no pun intended) to love these facts about myself. Being small, the violin fit me, and whenever I got jealous of tall girls with long legs, I would remind myself that muscular legs helped me excel in sports, which I loved to play anyway. The older I get, the more I find benefits to *all* of my characteristics, one being that they make me unique. Imagine that!

Lesson 3: Be a good person, stick to who you are, and in a haphazard way you serendipitously discover a lot of blessings that have accompanied you all along your journey.

I managed to survive school. While I was not the coolest kid, and while I *felt* different than others, I realized I was content being quiet on my own and just getting along with people. I stuck to just doing things I loved, minded my own business, and I did fine. As you get older, you realize that you were not the only one in school that just "cruised under the radar" as best as you could just to make it through. As you stumble along trying to find your place you trip over pebbles of embarrassment and run face first into accomplishments you didn't even see in front of you. Of course, I would find myself in new situations that pushed me out of my comfort zone or made me pray I wouldn't get into trouble. I also learned that being forced into something you didn't enjoy doing can sometimes be a blessing in disguise.

Joining Forensics . . . Not for Crimes and Death

While middle school shed some light on my differences, it simultaneously showcased new talents and interests. I never thought of myself as one who liked to do anything that required getting in front of people. It was simply a skill I didn't think I possessed.

One afternoon in sixth grade, my language arts teacher, Ms. Shannon, came up to me and mentioned an interest meeting for the forensics team. No, not a club that studies the science behind crimes and death. I guess I would describe it as a club where you could choose to compete as part of a debate team or compete by performing plays or short stories. It might be viewed as a "competitive theater club." You would compete in front of a group of people that included at least one judge and your fellow competitors.

"Why don't you just check out the meeting?" my teacher told me as she pulled me aside at the end of the class. I just politely smiled and sort of shrugged. I had no clue what she was talking about.

"Uhh, I don't know. Maybe."

"I think you would be good at it," she said in a convincing and encouraging tone. That got me suspicious. I gave her one of those "half smiles," where you curl both lips in toward your teeth.

"Sure, ok."

On a Wednesday after school, I found myself sitting in the meeting. I figured it wouldn't hurt just to sit there. I had *no* idea what I was getting into. I walked into the classroom and saw that there were a handful of other students there, unfortunately no familiar faces. I picked some seat in the middle, and just sat and waited for the meeting to start. The teacher in there was a total stranger to me, and my heart sank. I didn't know a soul in there. When the meeting began, the forensics coach, Ms. Whitaker, gave us a usual "Good afternoon, welcome," type of speech. She seemed friendly and excited enough. She gave a short description of things, and then popped in a VHS tape to show us some performances.

"*Is Ms. Shannon insane?*" my eyebrows rose up and my eyes got huge. "*Woman, what in your right mind sees me as someone who can perform in front of people and even more, have the ability to compete doing it? I barely talk in your class. Hell, I barely talk OUTSIDE of class!*" My jaw just dropped.

"*What have I done?*" I thought. "*Don't panic, just don't bring it up to Ms. Shannon in class, and move on. You don't have to do this. It was her suggestion, not requirement.*"

"How was it, the meeting?" were the first words Ms. Shannon greeted me with the next day. "Doesn't it sound neat?!"

"*Damn it, Ms. Shannon!*" I thought. "*Ugh.*" I was such a chicken and couldn't just tell her the truth. So, I came up with the most neutral nice words I could respond with.

"It was neat," was all I could think of. I kept walking to my seat avoiding eye contact in hopes of the conversation being over for at least forever. "*Way to officially screw yourself over, Nicole. You HAD to be nice.*"

Each day I worried Ms. Shannon would ask me about the club. In the beginning, I kept going to meetings for the sole purpose of having something to say in case she asked me anything. Pretending I was going to practices and then lying to her was no use. I wouldn't know what to lie about because I didn't know a thing about the forensics team! I have always loved reading, but never read plays or scripts, and forget trying to perform. I gave up on forcing my way through everything, and I eventually gathered up the guts to simply ask Ms. Whitaker for help. We decided it might be best to start competing in the category of "storytelling" instead. So, my journey began by telling children's stories.

I don't know how in the *hell* I managed to perform these pieces. I felt like an idiot standing up there doing what I thought was "performing." Early on, I was uncomfortable. I remembered the VHS tape Ms. Whitaker showed us, and I just kept praying she wouldn't record *us* and make us watch it to do some peer critiques. I tried my best to create voices and expressions for characters. Since you performed by yourself, you had to find ways to play all the characters. While I somehow managed not to pee on myself from my nerves, I gave everything I had in hopes that I was doing it properly. I figured I may as well give it my best because I would look ridiculous whether I tried hard or not. You feel silly enough talking to yourself as you switch back and forth between characters. When I performed, I heard my voice shaking and I felt my hands shaking.

Amazingly, I learned lesson #4 and picked up a few valuable nuggets of life tips along the way: It is possible to do anything that makes you want to shit yourself and simultaneously talk yourself through the panic. Mostly, I learned that will power, fear, and the mind are all amazing when they come together! A person can be brave in what feels like the most ridiculously scary moments. Of course, it requires you to throw yourself into the scary moment, but if you are ever brave enough (or forced) to try, you might surprise yourself!

Over the middle and high school years I found myself enjoying forensics even if I was still nervous performing. I even started to do what was called "double-enter" and compete in both storytelling and in humorous interpretation, performing comedy plays. I remember practicing a routine I heard on a cassette tape of comedians. It was called, *"The Chinese Waiter,"* performed by Buddy Hackett, a famous American comedian and actor. The piece involved a short-tempered, slightly inappropriate waiter at a Chinese restaurant trying to take the order of a group of Americans. To perform the piece, I dug deep for my "inner waitress with an attitude," personality and with my best Chinese accent I argued back and forth with my dinner guests about their meal orders. Memories of those forensics practices still make me smile. All I see is Ms. Whitaker literally in tears and my teammates rolling out of their desks howling with laughter every time that I practiced, *"The Chinese Waiter."* I loved the reaction, and in a way, the interaction with the audience. Best of all, I found a new love for making others laugh. I never thought I could do that.

Miley Cyrus Hit the High Note

What is the point of my telling all of this? Well, pardon the cheesiness, but the *experience* is my point. Back in her Disney days, Miley Cyrus had a song called "The Climb," where the theme is that it's not necessarily the destination that matters, but ultimately the journey. And there will always be challenges. We've all heard some aphorism of that nature, but it's true. The words in the song speak some kind of truth.

What did I REALLY get from forensics? I gained a new hobby that wasn't sports related. THAT was a miracle. Along with playing in the orchestra, participating in forensics reminded me of how much I love the arts and it fed the creative hunger I forgot I even had. I made new friends and got to travel. Becoming a more confident public speaker was another benefit. Not to mention the realization that I *could* speak in front of people! Finally, I learned a useful skill in real life – if something doesn't go "according to your script," don't panic, calmly move along (improvising if you absolutely must) and find your way back. If you've practiced enough, you can fall back on the basics and more importantly - you can trust yourself. That applies to performing of any kind, to playing sports, and even to failing at reaching goals in life. Life never follows a script, especially the one you write in your head, so figure out how to deal with it to reach your goal. It's important to understand, however, that it might mean admitting it was a bad day, and that someone else might have outdone you.

The courage I have does not always display itself in romantic ways, but it's in me. There is no way I could have ever grown as a person if I never took chances. The more I came across moments of embarrassment or failure, the more I realized that embarrassment is a part of life, but it's not the end of everything. The more you become comfortable with the fact that things might not go your way, the more open you are to both making and taking chances.

Forensics was never the most popular club in the schools where I lived. In fact, it was very likely that those of us on the forensics team where the only ones who really knew what the forensics team was. I was okay with that. I had found another hobby. I was happy. However, all good things must come to an end. Sort of.

"Most Likely To Succeed," Whatever That Means

So, fast-forward to post-graduate school, when was no longer 12, but 35 years old. I recall a few years ago when I was visiting home, I walked into my room and giggled at the sticker that I had placed on my bedroom door years ago. It was of the Geico lizard with an army helmet on his head. As I walked past the door, I tried to take it off and realized the sticker stuck too well. I couldn't take it off without those pesky white pieces still sticking to the door. No wonder why my mom screamed at me when I put it on the door. Whoops.

My room was untouched, the same furniture in the same arrangement; autographed Duke basketball posters on the wall (how many Tarheel enemies did I just gain?); and my graduation gowns left in my closet. On the bookcase sat some old yearbooks and Norman, a giant green stuffed rabbit my parents gave to me my first year in college. Our mascot at the University of NC in Charlotte was a "49er" named Norman, so that's what I named my rabbit.

My smile kind of faded as I looked at the old trophies and ribbons around the room. There were awards from when I was 10 years old, and even more recent years. They came from forensics tournaments, orchestra competitions, science fair projects, and various sports. I was voted "Most Likely to Succeed" and "Goofiest" my senior year in high school. I'll admit that I valued "goofiest" more than "most likely to succeed." Weird isn't it? But people thinking I was goofy simply took away the pressure to be "successful," and also made me feel like I stuck out less from my peers.

I wandered over to my window and I tried to peek through the blinds. I smiled as I remembered how my dad and I always have ridiculous arguments about the "proper way" to close the stupid blinds - angle them down, or angle them up? Anyway, I poked my fingers in between two dusty blinds. Looking outside, there was the familiar yellow fire hydrant on the corner. I saw my 12-year-old self still standing there with my violin case and those words replayed in my head.

"Don't worry, it'll pay off someday."

I felt a tiny bit of heartbreak chip away at the joy of reminiscing. I was pretty sure that "someday" was supposed to be before I turned 35. Hmmm, maybe my calculation was off. I went through the checklist in my head—high school diploma—got it; master's degree—got it; find job in good career field—I guess I did work my way into a teaching career, so...done. Hmmm, I'm still not finding where things went wrong. Uneasiness set in.

Why the heck can I not get myself steady in a career? I mean, I work hard. Here I was, now working two jobs, back in school, unable to pay my own rent.

Talk about being the "black sheep." Family gatherings meant sitting in a room where every adult was either retired or had completed school and been working in a steady career ever since. At some point I started to feel like anytime someone spoke with me, it was all small talk. If it didn't involve some promotion, getting married or being a new parent, it wasn't exciting.

"What's new with you, Nic?" someone would ask me.

"Same 'ol, same 'ol. Work, school. You know," I would reply, a little embarrassed knowing I had nothing very exciting to share. Some days I hoped *no* one would ask what's new with me. It was embarrassing, and I started to sense that after changing careers a few times, even news about changing careers was no longer exciting! It became the norm. While I was happy my family cared to ask how I was, I also wanted to hide when people were going around sharing what was new in their lives.

Now, I am part of an Asian family, and along with expectations like respecting elders, there were many others. I have come to appreciate that I am blessed with parents who have always pushed my brother and me to be our best, work hard, and keep faith at the top of the priority list. On that list is also strong family values and obtaining a good education. Each of these values has proven to ensure that while we may often have to tread some nasty waters in life, we will never drown.

However, what also deserves recognition is that my brother and I have parents who always support us and accept us for who we are. I would be lying if I said there was never a moment in time that I felt like the rest of the world thought I was supposed to be a doctor or something. Thank God Mom and Dad also let me roll around in the dirt, pick up a baseball, play the violin, *and* bang on drums. They always allowed room for me to explore every corner of my ambitious curious mind and heart. They provided a good balance of ass-busting *and* enjoying life.

As I looked at all the things in my room, I realized that all those dusty awards came with doing something I enjoyed. While I tried choosing careers that interested me, I think I took *"If you do what you love, you don't work a day in your life,"* a little too literally. I discovered two things: I probably tried TOO HARD to make my career from something I loved, and secondly, I have made myself too busy trying to hang on to *enjoying* the things I love. The more I caught myself stopping to literally tell myself, *"Remember to have fun,"* the more I worried. Enjoying something should not require you to remind yourself to enjoy it.

So here's the deal. I have all these awards—great. Ultimately, no one cares. Despite how good I might have been at something, I did not became a famous athlete, musician, actress, scientist, or famous anything.

I'm ok with that. What I realized I've missed most is the FUN I had doing these things - even if I was nervous, unsure, or just busy trying to fit in at the time. It's about "the climb" right?

Whatever trophies, wins, or losses that I earned, they just came along at the end of the experience. When I think about it, I'm glad that a lot of my hobbies are not my career. It takes the pressure off of "Most Likely To Succeed." I also think that having a hobby as a career would ironically have the potential to suck all the joy out of looking back and laughing at the memories.

People who have a career doing anything they truly love are blessed. I certainly give credit where credit is due, as making a dream a reality is *not* easy. Hey, if you are good at something you love, and you can make it into a successful career, I tip my hat to you! Every individual person is just that—a unique individual. Everyone has his or her own path to follow. Apparently, my path is all jacked up, and I have grown to embrace that. Even when frustrations come along, I have faith that there is beauty and purpose in my journey. In other words, many times I may hate my situation *in the moment*, but I know it's going to be ok. And once again, the most powerful reassurance is that even if I hate something in a moment, I can honestly say that I have no regrets whenever I look back, and no regrets no matter what other people believe. People usually only get a snapshot of the story anyway.

I think many people see the risks of using social media to place themselves on a scale of success. Often, we gravitate toward looking at posts of milestones, the "highest highs," and "lowest lows." And it's ok. After all, people on Facebook are called your "friends," right? You should share in their joys and their hard times. But remember that one event they post about doesn't cover all the months in between each post, and one picture is never the whole picture. I tend to post pictures of my pet fish, memes that make you lose brain cells (but still give you a daily dose of laughter), or news about my favorite sports teams. What you see on my Facebook page might not portray "Most Likely to Succeed," but hey, once a black sheep, always a black sheep.

God Has Got This . . .

At times I may "feel different" than others, whether I'm asked about my opinion on how to approach a problem, or even when I just stand in a room of people who might include my own family and friends. Ironically, in those moments, something in my gut also tells me I'm just as worthy of a person as anyone else. Maybe that's pride hanging on to me by two fingers, but I'll let it hang on and keep believing it. Over time I've learned to be patient with myself. I observe situations, and thoroughly think about how I will approach a problem or make a decision.

I proceed knowing that no matter what impression I make on others, preferably a positive one, I know my ultimate goal is Heaven. That ultimate goal reassures me to simply do what I think is right, and let God handle the rest. It often means that you must swallow pride when proving others wrong is what stands in the way of doing what is right. Some days you *must* give up, meaning let go and let God do the fighting. It doesn't mean you stop, but instead maybe you need to redirect, learn a tough lesson, take a breather, or do all three. I believe that if you keep God and Heaven in perspective as you work hard, then things will come together. Every road you travel has a purpose and if you keep your perspective open, every road has beauty. Do your thing and let everyone else worry.

One morning, when I lived in Houston, I sat in church listening to a homily given by the priest. Something he specifically said resonated with me:

When you seek to know God's dreams for you,
you develop good vision. You discover which talents, knowledge,
and experiences will give you your greatest fulfillment, because
he had these in mind when he created you. When you work hard
to make these dreams come true, forsaking distractions, persisting

past obstacles, and accepting the lessons that are hidden in hardships, you realize the best that life can offer.

I am learning that *why* you pick a road has a huge influence on the ultimate outcome. I think that with each career I have been a part of, I began with good intentions in my heart, but there was also a bit of selfishness or desire for self-glory hanging around in the background. While I tried not to let that be my driving force, I can certainly see its presence as I sit and ponder what sometimes appears to be only a messy glob of "career hopping." Maybe my intentions were not always perfect. How *stupid human* is that? Sometimes, it's hard, but the shameful acknowledgement that I was more selfish than I care to admit is a huge step in understanding my current path. What better time to bring up wandering sheep in the Bible?

...If a man has a hundred sheep and one of them goes astray, will he not leave the ninety-nine in the hills and go in search of the stray? And if he finds it, amen, I say to you, he rejoices more over it than over the ninety-nine that did not stray. In just the same way, it is not the will of your heavenly Father that one of these little ones be lost. [1]

Then so what if I'm a black or white sheep among the crowd? Who cares what others think about where I am on my journey? I've accepted that maybe my road through school and careers did not stay in the "box." My goal is Heaven. I believe that path is open to *anyone*, and therefore unique to *each* person. Oddly enough, sometimes when the craziness of this world begins to engulf me, and my path strays from the path of those voted "Most Likely to Succeed," the thing that keeps me going is knowing that people might see me as a "black sheep." It's convenient for me. I'm *supposed* to stray from the path.

Lord knows I've made mistakes and allowed the wrong reasons to influence my actions. However, I go to church because I make mistakes. God keeps me on track. My mistakes and his mercy are really what have brought me this far. Have you ever looked back at something and wondered how you ever made it through? Well... maybe you don't have to think too hard.

I still end up in uncomfortable situations, but hey, I'm still here, moving on. And to this day, I find myself occasionally still tugging around that exact same violin case with my pink bunny from middle school.

Embrace the Inner Black Sheep

One morning, I stood in the music room at church getting ready to play my violin for the mass. Participating in church gave me a chance to keep playing music. It also gave me the chance to give something back to the church.

As I packed up that old rental violin into the same hard case with the same little pink bunny attached to the handle, I looked up and smiled at the tie our pianist was wearing. The design was a bunch of sheep and one was colored in black.

I kind of smiled and said, "I like your tie." I did. I thought all the sheep were kind of cute.

He looked at me with a big grin and asked, "Well, have you found yourself? Which one are you?" He held out his tie so I could pick a sheep.

I couldn't help but smile really wide, and without hesitation pointed straight to the black one. "That one! All the time!" Instead of fidgeting with my violin case and blurting out in my defense about being different, I had a happy kind of confidence. I am who I am with a lot of gifts to share, some gifts greater than others. The point is that I could try to make giant accomplishments from every little thing, or I could simply choose to give my best in whatever way that I can. Take playing music at church for example. I've done worse things than hit wrong notes playing music. If God can forgive me for being judgmental or selfish, then I think he will likely forgive me for misplacing my fingers on the violin every now and then. Hey, the Bible says make a joyful noise, not necessarily perfectly performed one!

I can choose to focus on getting to a place where there is no concern for the value of money, or trophies, to a place where no one cares about how many "likes" you have on Facebook, and no one keeps count of how many people you impress. That sounds like a nice stress-free deal. It kind of sounds like Heaven. It's got nothing to do with reaching the top of the mountain, and everything to do with how I utilize the time, chances, and gifts God so abundantly gives me.

The same priest I quoted earlier also stated, *"When you give what you can give, God will do what God does."*

Sounds fair to me, because all that I have to give was ultimately God's to begin with. I'm pretty sure God does amazing things as long as you trust him.

The Backwards Bucket List

My journey in life thus far has taken me all over the place. I wrote a song called "Postcard From the Moon," where I refer to my journey as writing a "backwards bucket list." What I mean is that I don't always focus on trying to "check off" a list of all the things I want to do. I often find myself having done things I never imagined I would do *before* I even have time to look at the things I *want* to do.

In fourth grade, I was busy dreaming about my goal to be a famous tennis player. By college, I found myself studying to be an architect. Then, when I became a teacher instead, my journey to find a better place to teach led me to completing paramedic school and working on an ambulance, and as a physical therapist technician for a moment in time. My record is something like 0 wins -50 losses in terms of ending up anywhere I "planned" to go. But each time I ended up somewhere, I experienced something amazing. I met goals I didn't even know I had and walked away with no regrets because I always gave my best efforts.

Oh the opportunities, gifts, and lessons I have come across through the grace of God! Those chances came in the form of everything from starting IV's in the back of an ambulance, to sharing a pack of peanut butter crackers with someone having a bad day. It has been made clear to me that even though I have not had a consistent career, there was always worthy work to be done. In the midst of that work, I had the blessing to explore personal weaknesses and strengths I never knew existed and discover the strength of God within me. Now THAT'S a journey, and this little black sheep is going to keep skipping along knowing that it is going to be worth it.

5

SHIT HAPPENS, AND SOMETIMES IT HITS THE FAN

❧

I was jogging down the path soaking up the gorgeous fall weather in Houston, Texas. It was not exactly "cool and crisp" as much as it was just not hot. I figured a little exercise and fresh air would do me some good. It always helps when I'm a little stressed. With each step I heard the crunch of the tiny pebbles under my sneakers, and I smiled because that sound always reminds me of my cleats stepping onto the field when I played Little League Softball. As I rounded the corner of the trail, I glanced to the right and saw the amphitheater that sat in the middle of the park. I thought about when I first moved to Houston and how excited I was to live so close to the park. I would have easy access to the free shows. While I still enjoyed the park a year after moving there, I realized that on this day, the grand picture of my current situation clouded that once eager, dream-chasing, optimistic "living in a new big city" kind of attitude.

As I mentioned, I've been a bit of a "career-hopper," and at this point it had been a year since my pursuit of a career as a firefighter was exchanged for a second shot at teaching as a career. That's how I ended up in Texas. In the end, that shot I took reminded me why I love teaching. Unfortunately, it also reminded me why I first left teaching. And so here I was, jogging and once again trying to figure out what I was doing with my life. At this point, I settled for a part-time tutoring job (sound familiar?) while shifting back into the first responder career field, studying to become a paramedic. Something in my gut told me that while a career on an ambulance may stir my excitement, curiosity, and desire to help others, it didn't quite stir my soul.

While I continued to jog, I started talking to myself.

"Ok, you've got $16.72 left in your checking account, about a thousand left in your emergency fund. That's not bad compared to many other situations. Thank, God." I glanced up making sure I remembered to count my blessings before I unleashed my list of not so great things. "You just need to think carefully about how to dip into that fund," I advised myself. Part-time tutoring paid well, but not well enough. "Let's see… electricity bill, internet, insurance. Oh, duh, a few groceries and next week's gas." I blew a sigh through my lips, kind of sounded like a horse. "Oh boy." I tried to focus for a moment on the "crunch" sound under my feet.

"Happy place, happy place," I thought as I began to fight a frown forming on my face. "Stop. Frowns are bad for wrinkles." I lifted my eyebrows. I looked up and realized the jogger I just passed said hi. I think he read my eyebrows as saying hello.

"Focus, Nicole! Remember, you are blessed . . . I will not let my situation bring me down. Not gonna happen." The more I said that, the more I worried. I knew I was not happy at the moment. It is amazing how there can be a change in the way you see the world, or dare I say a change within *yourself,* when you become entangled in inevitable life transitions. Ah, yes, the internal battles we put ourselves through to live the life we want to live. There is that fight

between who we *want* to be, who we *should* be, and who we *are in the moment.*

There is a famous saying - "life happens." The ugly version is expressed as, "shit happens." People often use the expression "life happens" to get themselves to carelessly shrug and put one foot in front of the other to keep on moving through whatever mud they are trudging (i.e., unfortunate circumstances or events). Well, as I jogged to the music of my thoughts wrestling, I slowly began to add another element to its interpretation. Life happens, *because* life happens. Hopefully, you come across things in life simply because you are trying to *do* something in life.

Those fall days in Texas, I often reminded myself that my bank account and my constant job search were simply the facts of the moment. These were the circumstances of the risks I knew I'd be taking with each career change and leap of faith.

"Today my circumstances have become the facts that I am determined to make sure will never be permanent in my life," I grumbled to myself and tried to run faster in hopes that it would help me push tears back. Remember my movie montage? Well, this was a great moment for the music to blast in. I knew God's will would never steer me wrong. I also knew that I was driven to get somewhere. To quiet down the "noise" of my thoughts I once again just told myself, "I'm just trying to get to Heaven, that's it, just

Heaven. Just keep moving." I tried again to focus on the crunch sound under my feet.

Another popular saying, often credited to John Lennon is, "Life is what happens while you're busy making plans." However, for me, instead of "while you're making plans," it's more like, "Life happens while crap is hitting the fan, and you desperately try to clean it up." Well, if the world keeps spinning no matter your circumstances, there were many days I just wanted the fan to stop spinning.

Let's not forget though, that in the midst of all the visible crap getting flung around, things *are* happening. This would include *good* things! As I continued listening to the crunch of the sand under my feet, I continued my conversation with myself.

"Ok," I took a deep breath and began to talk myself through the stress. "The good 'ol checklist… my goals moving to Texas: grow as a teacher, (it was a blessed second chance); meet my future husband, and work on this martial arts program I've always dreamed of…" I kind of laughed.

"Well," I said, "I guess one out of three isn't bad considering my circumstances." I smiled to myself as I hit a positive note. I did get to run a martial arts club alongside my friend, Harris. While it was short-lived, there were many small, yet profound successes to be thankful for. The hope that I helped some kids stay out of trouble and helped others gain even the slightest bit of confidence made me feel optimistic. Thinking about it just made me smile while I was jogging along the trail. My reality was that I have gone almost every direction AWAY from the hopes I brought to Texas. If that's not a life transition, I don't know what is.

The amazing thing is that I look at the chapters in this book prior to this one, (which were written a year or so earlier), and I see the SAME hopeful spirit in me . . . but I am a just a bit older, and a bit more experienced. By "experienced" I don't mean "been there, done that." Rather, I've learned that my own stubbornness can result in getting kicked while I am already down. I learned that among many things, I need to rely more on a strong faith rather than on my own dumb decisions. One of the biggest lessons I've recently learned is that despite my constant push to always move forward, I am also pretty good at holding myself back.

Meddling in Mediocre, Let Go, and Let God

While in Texas, I began to discover a not-so-great pattern and attitude within me that I seemed to circle around. That pattern was that I often settled for being mediocre in my efforts. It also became apparent in the way I let others treat me (which, again, ultimately turns into how I treat myself). There were times I knew that people did not take me seriously. The sad part was that

I just settled for it and didn't bother to show them any differently. I was infuriated whenever I knew I could do better than I did, whether it was playing music, training in martial arts, or anything else. I didn't want people to think I was not good at something, and yet I didn't care to try harder. I don't even know why. However, I hated how my lack of confidence gave people a reason to doubt my abilities. And it is my own dumb fault. I realized that lately, I did my best gritting my teeth to get through a lot, but not my best in whatever the actual task was. It scared me to think that I would regret it if I didn't change that attitude.

Have you ever regretted giving a puny effort toward something? There is disappointment in knowing that you could have given more of yourself to something that you already gave your time. There are bigger things to worry about than impressing others. Ok, fair enough, except it shouldn't be an *excuse* for not trying your best. "Life happens," *should never* be an excuse.

If anyone *actually* came after me to kill me, a mediocre effort in martial arts would only get me killed. I can't defend or attack in slow motion just so I could look like I'm in a movie doing it. Mediocre won't cut it. So that fan with spinning crap hitting it has one benefit - it goes in a circle. As a result, it brought to my attention a problem that until recently, I never realized was hiding quietly in my presence. Life happens, but sometimes you can't shrug your shoulders and just move on.

People say you need to let go of the past. I discovered that your mind can play tricks on itself with that mentality. Not that letting go is a bad thing. However, there is a blurry area between "letting go," and being in denial. If it's not denial, then maybe you just suppress something so well, that while it doesn't bother your daily living, it certainly holds back good potential. When that truth reveals itself, **THAT,** my friend can become the crap that hits the fan. Sometimes you think you've let go of something, when in fact down the road you find that that something has been tiptoeing behind you all this time. One day you realize that every time that problem has presented itself, you might have found a way to compromise your potential to do or be great. You become a pro at working around what you are trying to avoid, convincing yourself you are dealing with the problem. You meddle in mediocre because mediocre becomes a comfort zone.

So, do you face the obstacle like a badass? Do you move on and know that one day you'll get over it? Do you pray about it? In my opinion all of these approaches work together if you can keep yourself mentally and spiritually together. I believe in giving all my troubles to God. However, in doing so, I have still got to do *my* part in putting one foot in front of the other.

* * *

It was not until I began school to be an EMT that I realized two very important things. Number one, I wasn't over all of what happened with John. To be clear, I am referring to the incident described in the chapter "Blast On." Number two, I do hold myself back more than I want to admit to myself, and I ain't very proud of that. It wasn't until sometime later, I discovered that maybe I was a little more affected by my past with John than I knew. The good news was that I was affected in negative *and* positive ways.

Life happens . . .don't let it slip away or be ruined before you realize any damage you might bring upon yourself. And don't let "life" draw you away from the things you love. If it does, that's a sign you need to step back and work on some self-care. There is no shame in that.

One semester, while working through the paramedic program, a requirement for students was to see a counselor for at least a couple of sessions. Our clinicals posed the risk that we could come across some disturbing calls while on duty in an ambulance. During our first round of clinicals, none of my calls on the ambulance had been too extreme, so I didn't see much need to talk to a counselor. However, since sessions were required, I had to at the very least show up. I could talk about anything I wanted or needed to, as long as I attended the required sessions.

In my first session with the counselor (I'll call her Ms. T) I walked into her office thinking nothing of it. The room looked like any ordinary office, a desk with a computer, two chairs, and a few things hanging on the wall.

"Hello," Ms. T said in a friendly tone. "Hi," I replied.

We went through the usual "How are you" and "why you're here" conversation. She was a nice lady. Then Ms. T handed me a clipboard with a piece of paper.

"I'd like for you to fill out this simple questionnaire. It's confidential, so don't worry. It basically gives me an idea about you. I'll give you a few minutes and feel free to ask any questions if you need."

"Sure," I said taking the clipboard she handed me from the other side of her desk. I put my backpack on the floor, double checked that my cell phone was on silent, and got to work. It sort of jostled my memory of the counseling session I tried after the incident with John. But I thought that a questionnaire was easy enough to do. If anything, working on it would take up some time. Noooo problem. I felt a sudden moment of uneasiness as a quick picture of sitting in the therapist's office several years ago suddenly flashed in my mind.

Some of these questions were kind of similar. But I told myself that this session was not *that* session. It was about five years later, and a totally different scenario. *"Hmm, I guess surveys are some kind of standard procedure for starting therapy or something."* Like a cartoon character shaking away the stars spinning around his head, I shook it off and refocused on the clipboard in my hand.

After several general questions about things like hobbies and medical history, I came across a section with direct yes/no responses, that covered experiences like the death of a loved one, homelessness, and physical/sexual/emotional abuse or harassment. I stopped and stared. I wanted to put "yes" for sexual harassment, but I wasn't quite sure if I "qualified." Was my history of this occurrence "bad enough" to mark "yes"? I mean, I was over it, wasn't I? I just stared at the paper and contemplated. I looked at the counselor, and she was sitting quietly doing things on her computer as she waited for me.

"I mean other people have legitimately been raped or continuously abused, right?" I thought to myself. *"My one incident with John isn't really that big of a deal, is it?"* I looked up hesitating to ask Ms. T to clarify the question on the paper. She was looking over some paper in front of her. *"Nevermind,"* I thought, *"it's all old stuff anyway."*

I skipped the question and decided to come back to it. When I handed the paper to the counselor, I felt like an uncomfortable squirmy kid handing the teacher my quiz and waiting for results. She smiled and showed me the paper.

"You skipped one," she said pointing at the question.

"Damn it," I thought. I hoped she would leave it alone if I left it blank. I became embarrassed and could feel myself growing hot as I began to discover that I think maybe I *wanted* to mark "yes" all along. But, I still wasn't sure if I should.

"Oh," I mumbled, "Yeah, I wasn't really sure what to put there. I mean, there was a small incident a while ago." I shrugged my shoulders. "I mean I think it's fine though."

"Ok, well, does it ever bother you sometimes? Even just cross your mind every now and then?"

I paused. I honestly didn't know the answer to that question. Or maybe I did. I shrugged but made sure I was still sitting up and speaking clearly.

"Um," I seriously had no clue what to say. *"Just say yes or no, Nicole, don't make it so complicated. Don't be so stupid dramatic…"*

"I mean I guess, but not really," I answered. *"Ugh, nice going. You played that off really well,"* I sighed to myself and felt my shoulders drop at the same time.

"You know," she said, "we'll put yes, just in case." She made circling "yes" on the paper look so simple of a task.

"Ok," I said, a little bit embarrassed. "That works."

Crap Hit the Fan, but That's a Good Thing

By our second session, Ms. T and I had been talking about different activities I enjoyed and ways I could get involved in those activities. I was new to the city and trying to meet people and find ways to enjoy my hobbies was sometimes a bit of a challenge for me. Ms. T pointed out online resources and ways to find social groups with similar interests. At some point I mentioned my love for martial arts and how I once ran a club for my students. Somehow the conversation worked its way into how I struggled to find a place for myself to continue training.

"I don't know, sometimes it's just difficult for me to motivate myself to participate, even though I know I want to. Maybe it's the testosterone in the air, heh," I offered a small joke.

"Like *how* is it difficult?" Ms. T asked, more concerned than amused.

"Mmmmm," I was trying to think how to describe what I felt. "It's sometimes like there's a buildup of anxiousness when I train." I did my best to describe it, but I struggled. Ms. T just patiently waited.

"Maybe it's like some mental block. A lot of times I will drive to the school to train and as I get to the turn from the street, I get nervous. So I just keep on driving." I realized how bad that sounded.

"Where do you go instead?"

"I just go home. Disappointed. Sometimes I get as far as actually parking at the school to train," I started, almost proud to claim it. "Then I just sit there, and eventually pull out of the spot and drive home." That didn't come out as brave as I thought it would sound. "I just get real nervous before I get out of the car, so I just tell myself to go home because it's not worth feeling this way." I was still embarrassed, but I had to admit to myself as I sat there, that it felt *really* good to tell someone all of this.

"Ok," Ms. T said. "How about when you do get into class and train, do you enjoy it?"

I sat there and thought for a moment. It's funny how you can let a million thoughts and words race through your head, when you know all you need is one word to answer a question.

"Yes, I mean, I *try* to anyway. I mean, I *really* love learning and training. And I tell myself to calm down, that I should be proud to be standing there even though I am nervous. Being able to just walk into the building is an accomplishment, right?" I looked down at her desk.

I wasn't looking at anything in particular, my eyes just moved down as I started to think.

I began to feel a little frustrated. It broke my heart that something I enjoyed so much was so difficult to enjoy. I felt a rush of sadness as I realized how much I missed my old school back home and everybody I used to train with, my old friends. It was annoying how my favorite way to relieve stress was the one thing that stressed me out the most. Everything I described was accurate. The complete truth was that I *did* enjoy training, and I knew that I had the ability to really progress as a martial artist. I wanted to. However, nine times out of ten when I did get into class to train, it wasn't without at least one moment of debating throwing up, and it was never without thinking at least once that I wanted to go home. Maybe it did have to do with all the testosterone in the air, a discomfort being around males always wanting to "up" one another or show off. By the way, this in no way means I generalize and put all male martial artists in a negative category. There are plenty of kind and humble people you come across when you train.

As I sat there thinking about everything and hoping Ms. T would give me something encouraging to walk out with, a lightbulb finally went off—I had a problem. These feelings, my actions, were not normal, *especially* for me. Life happens, right? So why have I not moved on even though I have physically moved away from the problem?

As I heard myself talking to Ms. T, I began to hear actions and characteristics I didn't want to be a part of me. I was kind of disappointed in myself for not realizing this sooner. At this point it was more like I was able to almost see myself from the outside. I began to notice how I felt around people even outside of training, and especially when I was by myself with anyone. There was discomfort. I gave every effort to be friendly no matter what. But in the back of my mind, I held up the strongest guard I could. I might be hanging out with people, asking someone for help in a store, or chatting with someone at church. It usually pertained to males. He could be older, younger, super good-looking, average-looking, any race, homosexual, heterosexual, and he could be standing right there next to his wife. He could be someone I've known for a long time, or a complete stranger. Even now that I was in a new city, and several states away from John, it didn't change anything. Sometimes there was a sense of uneasiness, but I never wanted to run away from a situation because I refused to let my past dictate how I live my life. And I certainly did not want to take anything out on kind people. Part of me is very glad I am hard-headed enough to push myself that way. However, once I started to see the light, it didn't even matter. Was this REALLY a problem of mine? As much as I didn't like it, I started to believe it was real. At that point all I cared about was making things better, about helping myself get back to normal. This just wasn't me, and I didn't want to be this uncomfortable forever. As much of an introvert as I can be, I generally love being around people.

The weird thing was that as much as seeing some truth come to the light worried me, it also gave me a sense of relief. There was no magic formula or "fix-it" medicine but talking really did help. So, quick public service announcement—if you (the reader) know in your gut that you need to get something off your precious heart PLEASE do. Find SOMEONE reliable to talk to. You'll find there is no shame when you realize how much better you will feel. It's not easy to do, but it's worth it. Be patient with yourself, but most importantly, be HONEST with yourself.

"I give myself credit every time I walked through the doors and onto the mat to train." I continued my talk with Ms. T. "It takes a lot to get to that point and I don't want to leave class if I made it that far." I sat there and pictured myself lined up for training and participating in warm-ups. I would give a loud "kihap" (that "hi-ya" scream everyone mocks when they "do karate") with every warm-up punch and tried to make myself enjoy being in class again. But deep down I knew I was simply going through the motions, putting more effort into working on calming down my racing heart. I knew that the louder I would kihap, the more nervous I was. The scream helped get jitters out of my system.

I hated it.

"*Suck it up, Nicole. You belong here.*" I would think to myself as I just followed along with the movements of the other students. "*Stand up tall, you deserve to be here. Just give it time, and you'll see.*"

"Let me ask you something." I snapped out of my little flashback, sat up, and looked at Ms. T. "Do you want to continue to stand up strong and fight this?"

"*Now you're talking,*" I thought. I was taking it as a compliment, you know, that I was being tough and fighting through my battle. This was the encouragement and recognition I needed to hear. I have been fighting through this for so long. I was able to pick my head up and look up, ready for what Ms. T was going to say.

"OR," she continued.

"*OR? There's another option here?*" My pride skidded to a halt.

"Do you want to move forward?" she asked.

"*Yikes,*" I thought. I stared as my "balloon head" slowly deflated and my eyes drifted downwards again. Well, there it was. In that instant I took on a whole new perspective. I realized that up until then I believed that "being a fighter" and "getting through this" *was* moving forward. It was certainly a step. However, looking at how and when Ms. T presented her question, I realized that the fight I was fighting only kept me in a cycle. Like the shit hitting the fan, I kept going in circles of a mess I *thought* I was cleaning up. I counted every martial arts class I made it through as a "win" in my head. But now, it almost appeared to me as if I were bullying myself. I kept coming back for more, and I didn't need to. I compromised my love for something; I compromised my potential to grow in something; I compromised my well-being. Going to class didn't solve my problem. Maybe trying my best to be brave isn't bad, and perhaps it was a good step, but what direction was that step taking me?

The Warrior

There is a book I read, *On the Warrior's Path*, by Daniele Bolelli. In one chapter, he talks about two perspectives a person can take when faced with conflict. The idea is that seeing adversity and tolerating it is very different than discerning what it is you are struggling with.[1] It's similar to Ms. T's question, is it a matter of standing strong and fighting, or moving forward? Do you remember my friend Harris who helped me with the martial arts club? I talk to him every now and then, and it is inevitable that the topic of martial arts will work its way in. We once chatted about how there are approaches to martial arts that often parallel combat to life itself. Harris said:

> *I believe the greatest display of conflict is actually not seen...*
> *It's very subtle, it starts with understanding yourself, then*
> *you'll be able to see the intentions of others...martial arts*
> *can train this awareness in our own muscles and therefore*
> *our brains in a physical and conscious sense. That's why it*
> *takes so long for us to get over trauma...because it becomes*
> *physically embedded in us. Martial arts is one of the few*
> *disciplines that the physical can reach the mentality in very*
> *positive and life-changing ways.*

Life happens, right? We *all* have some kind of battle going on, and to each person, his or her particular battle is their focus; it takes over their world. It may mean nothing to you, but it means everything to that person. It took a while, and I did not realize it at the time, but looking back I learned that yes, how we deal with our situation says a lot about ourselves to others. However, it is even more amazing how much it teaches *you* about yourself. Even years later, if you are willing to, you can take an old situation and reopen a wound to study it not with anger or frustration, but instead with bravery, curiosity, humility, and heart. Doing so has an insane potential to help you learn and grow.

Martial arts is amazing that way, and I find that it really does apply to everything you do. Yes, there is the element of resilience. Yes, there is the realization that practice can make you better. However, I am also talking about applying the mental and emotional element. I think it's almost like one can develop a "sixth sense." You gain an ability to feel a situation and learn how to move with and through it. You sometimes even find yourself talking yourself through it. It's similar to how I learned to face my fear when I was new to the forensics team. You realize you *can* focus and think your way through if you are determined enough in the midst of the chaos.

If you get knocked down enough times you soon realize that jumping right back up energized by anger or worse, *pride*, will only get you knocked back down before you even understand your battle. The more experienced you become, the more you are also willing to lose in order to gain a deeper understanding of whatever you are trying to learn about. You begin to place a value on understanding your situations, obstacles, "enemy," and even yourself. In other words, you're not afraid to lose a few rounds for the sake of the bigger picture.

Then there is the element of trusting yourself and your training. I describe it well in the next chapter. I learned it best when I practiced breaking boards with a spinning kick. You practice technique, timing, generating power, and judging distance all the time. However, my biggest lesson was that there is a key moment, literally a *split-second* right before you spin to kick that you must switch off your brain. If I don't stop thinking in that split second, the science of the kick clouds up my concentration, and all of my focus disappears. My brain goes from screaming, "KICK!" to re-analyzing distance, speed, height. And just like that, the energy I've built up is drained, and I must start over. When you commit, you commit.

Martial arts teaches you about not quitting, about persevering. It teaches you that although it is a factor, size is not the *determining* factor in any battle. Many martial arts schools have tenets posted on a wall. I once trained at school in North Carolina (shoutout AIM family!). The instructors always made it a point to connect training with the tenets – courage, integrity, perseverance, self-control, and indomitable spirit. Without a doubt, indomitable spirit was my immediate favorite.

Oh, Yeah?! Well, My Mom Said . . .

One summer, when I was about 6 or 7 years old, I was heading home from tennis camp with my brother. We were riding down the road in my dad's old sky-blue Monte Carlo. My mom was driving, and my brother and I were in the back seat. I looked back as we were driving away from the big "Iron Mike," statue, an icon for Ft. Bragg, North Carolina. We pulled up to a stoplight, and I couldn't sit still. Those leather seats are not forgiving in the summer heat! I kept moving around trying to find a new position and ended up bending my knees and sort of sitting on my feet. While we waited at the light, my mom looked up into the rearview mirror and out of nowhere opened her mouth.

"I'm going to tell you guys something. You probably won't remember this tomorrow, but I promise you that you will someday." I thought she was about to lay it on me for moving so much in the backseat, and I started to sink down and freak out. Now she was right, for like the next ten years her words never crossed my mind. But man, to this very day, do they resonate in every life battle I come across. I nervously caught mom's eyes as I glanced into the rearview mirror.

"You should never fight with your muscles," she said. "You fight with your brain. Ok?" I sat there staring back into the rearview mirror as my mom's eyes looked into it through her giant glasses. Thinking as deep as any 7-year-old could think, I replied.

"Ok!" Then I looked out the window hoping I would catch a blue Volkswagen Beetle so I could punch my brother in the arm. Blue buggies were worth two punches.

"You remember that when you get bigger," Mom said. It creeps me out how vividly I remember that moment in the car. Years later, Mom would still bring up her point—If you lose an arm or a leg, you can still live. If the brain and mind are lost, there is very little—if anything—that you can do. Understanding a situation and every factor involved, plays a major role when you are faced with a challenge. Muscles don't solve problems, thinking does.

I have always valued this lesson, and I've always tried to live by it. It took me a while to really understand what it meant, but as it became clearer, the advice has served me well. However, I will say that this battle of mine, which ironically involves martial arts, has been extremely challenging. I stand by mom's advice. After all that has happened in the past several years, I see even more how your mental well-being and inner peace can be so much more valuable than solely a healthy diet or exercise. Take care of your mind and never take it for granted. Your brain along with your mindset is WAY more powerful than any muscles you can ever strengthen. Your mind is what makes you completely give up, not your muscles.

* * *

One morning after a session with Ms. T, I sat in my car before EMT class and needed a way to just vent. I was exhausted in many ways, and since talking to her, I now had more on my mind. Well, I grabbed my notebook and pen and just started to write:

Only when you directly face your shadow, will the sun actually light your way. From there, it's not time to shadow box, it's time to walk in the direction the light guides you. You don't need to think about where you're going. Sometimes the first step is to simply walk on. Eventually, the shadow will move out of the way, as long as you persist. See, it's not solely about being a fighter. The question isn't "who is going to win this fight-me, or you?" No, the question is, "Do I want to fight, or do I want to move forward?" This does not mean to bury a problem deep inside. In fact, the process of moving forward is just the opposite. Acknowledge a problem. Try to understand the most important part(s) of the millions of reasons, excuses, and analyses your precious, troubled heart and beautiful mind dance around. However, do not waste time dwelling, because before you know it YEARS will have passed and even if you have moved on because the rotating Earth forced you to move, you may one day realize that the obstacle you thought you overcame was really just tagging along quietly, possibly even holding you back. Then one day you wake up saying it's all good, I'm gonna "warrior" my way through this . . . but the old ball and chain slowly start to weigh you down as you begin to realize you still have some shadows you must deal with.

And speaking of the rotating Earth, what a blessing! I don't just mean the gift of each day to try again. I mean the inevitable push you have no control over. Yes, you may wake up YEARS LATER to find you still have an issue to address, but first, appreciate all the days the good Lord has presented you with so that you CAN keep moving. He must keep you around for something, so your ass better get to work! Secondly, there is no excuse. It's a hard truth, but as they say, the world keeps on spinning with or without you. So, you better get moving!"

So, there you go. Life sure does happen. As I move on, I wouldn't say that I wasted precious martial arts time altogether. I was just doing some necessary healing. However, as life happens and steers you off your "planned route," it's important not to forget about the little lessons, beauties, blessings, and opportunities that are *SO VERY* present amidst all the suddenly magnified crap you can easily bury yourself in. God squeezes his way into EVERYTHING, especially in your worst experiences. He uses it to reveal *and* help you grow in strength and in faith. He is present, even if you are in the middle of deciding whether or not you BELIEVE he is. That's how awesome he is. Life happens because "life happens." Sometimes crap will hit the fan, but sometimes that's also known as a wakeup call. Don't ignore it. Don't let life pass you by because you are too busy dealing with it, or because you never dealt with it in the first place.

6

PUCKER FACTOR

🎵

Capsizing? Go for it!

Through experience, you start to see how some goals are best accomplished if you just follow through. Take for example, learning how to swim. You can hang onto the edge of a pool and practice kicking your feet every day. Even if you develop your muscles, it isn't until you let go of the wall and actually begin to submerge yourself that you learn how to _swim_. Sometimes you've got to learn the hard way.

I remember one time in college, sitting a kayak talking about the steps for doing a "wet exit," which is basically how to escape if you capsize while you're secured in the kayak. I wasn't too nervous about physically practicing the steps we had learned. To begin with, we were in a swimming pool and we had the comfort of the presence of our instructors around us. I waited patiently, bobbing up and down in my bright orange kayak, and eventually, it was my turn.

"Alright, Nicole, are you ready to try it?" I turned and saw my instructor heading toward me.

"I think so, yup!" I was excited and knew I had a grin on my face. I had been eagerly watching my peers do their practice wet exit.

"What do we do now?" the instructor asked as he pushed his way through the water towards my kayak.

"Hug the kayak, hit it hard three times, lift skirt, and get out." I listed the steps we were taught.

"Awesome!" he said. "Here we go!" I heard a thud on the kayak, felt a push, and before I knew it, I found myself upside down in the pool. Within a couple of seconds, I was surrounded by swirls of water and bubbles. The comfort of my initial big breath quickly became the feeling of the pressure of the water going up my nose, followed by that stinging sensation you get in your nasal/sinus area. Just like that, I realized that I had better calm down before I just gasp and take in all water. I followed every step perfectly, but I'd be lying if I said I was totally comfortable sitting upside-down underwater and stuck inside a kayak. *"Don't breathe just yet!"* I told myself. *"Hug the kayak, hit hard three times!"* I wanted to breathe in so bad. *"This so dumb, I just wanna pull the skirt and get out! Who invented the first two steps in a wet exit anyway? Dumbass!"* I angrily grasped the kayak and hit it three times, listening to the sound of the muffled "thuds" under water. My hand stung from hitting the kayak so hard. I then felt a wave of calm cross my mind as I found the tab on the skirt, easily lifted it, and got my legs out of the kayak. I pushed aside the kayak wanting to kick the stupid thing and with relief got my head above water.

"Nice work!" I heard someone say. It took me a few seconds, but I then remembered the instructor was literally a few feet from me and he was standing in chest-high water. "Ready for the next one?"

"No!" I thought. "Sure thing," I said. "That was kind of crazy."

"Different when you're actually in the water, isn't it?"

"For sure."

While I knew the steps and tried to calmly follow them, there was a wave of panic the second I processed the fact that I was upside down, holding my breath, and sealed into a kayak. The only way out was through. After two or three runs, a wet exit started to become a bit more of a natural process. Practice helps you learn procedures, but experience teaches you about all the elements of a situation.

* * *

"Alright, Nicole and Jim, you ready? You're up!"

I almost choked on the water I was trying to chug. "*WHOA! WAIT, WHAAA??*" I thought.

"Grab your gear, oxygen, TIC, halligan, whatever you need," our instructor said. "Let's go, let's go, people are dying up there waiting on you!"

Jim, who was leaning up against the fire truck next to me, bent over to pick up his O2 tank.

"Alright, let's do this," he said as he started walking.

"Aw, man, I didn't wanna go first," I whispered to him so our instructor didn't hear. We were running practice drills. I just started training as a volunteer firefighter, and while I was eager to get started, I admit that when it came to a new drill, I preferred to watch others and learn from their mistakes before I gave it a go.

"Meeee either," Jim responded. "What do you want this go round – TIC or halligan?" He held up the thermal imaging camera and the halligan in each hand. I was working on getting my gloves on.

"Damn Mickey Mouse gloves," I thought pulling on my gloves. I called them that because they were huge on my hands, like Mickey Mouse's gloves. While my chief had tried to find the smallest gear he could, it wasn't easy, and since training began ASAP, I had no time to wait for special order gear. Being just under 5' tall, hovering around a whopping 108 pounds, any gear I put on was well over a couple sizes too big. I wasn't exactly what you'd expect to see on a firefighter calendar. "Halligan," I said nodding toward my favorite "weapon of choice" for equipment. Mike, another trainee, came over, stood in front of me, and grabbed one strap hanging from the bottom left of the O2 pack on my back. Jim grabbed the strap on the bottom right. They stood in front of me grinning. "Ready?" he said as he grinned at Jim. I started to chuckle.

"Ready," Jim said smiling. "Hold on, lil' bit," he said to me as I made sure my feet were planted. "PULL!" I stood my ground as Jim and Mike gave a huge tug on the straps. My classmates always got a kick out of giving the extra tug on my O2 pack straps. The gear on me was so big and that extra tug just ensured that I got the straps as tight as possible. I tied the straps so they wouldn't be hanging down to my ankles and grabbed the halligan.

"Let's go, slowpokes! People are waiting up in that building!" Jim and I looked at each other, irritated, but more likely so because we knew the instructor was right, even if this was just a rescue drill and the "people" were actually rescue dummies. I looked up and saw light smoke sneaking its way out of the second-story window. Practice how you want to perform, right? For the drill, the fire came from barrels that were distributed throughout the building and contained burning wood. There was enough to create the realistic effect of smoke and make it tough to see.

Entering the field of first responding I knew there would be a great responsibility to help others in stressful situations, but of course, being excited and young, I guess I just assumed I'd just never have to deal with these situations. This day, I learned otherwise pretty quickly.

So here I was, standing before a search and rescue drill. It was the "meat and potatoes" of what the world thinks of when they hear "firefighter" – the smoking building, climbing the ladder to rescue people inside. Jim and I briskly walked toward the building. I grabbed the rung (step) a few up from the bottom of the ladder that was laying on the ground, with all my might got a running start dragging the ladder, and slung that thing so the feet of the ladder hit the base of the building.

"That's what I'm talking about y'all," I heard one of the instructors say. "Y'all see that? When it comes down to it, you just do what you gotta do to get the job done, slide and throw that ladder if it's the only way you can move it quick enough." My confidence got the much-needed boost as I was made a positive example to the class. However, as confident as I was, there was a hint of uneasiness that there was always someone in the class watching me and second guessing my abilities. I hustled to the other end, picked up the ladder, and began to "walk it up" to stand, raise, and position it. I placed the ladder and kind of stared at it for a moment, a bit unsure. I couldn't quite remember what we had learned about positioning the ladder. I secured it as best as I could, and Jim started walking up. I shrugged assuming that if Jim had no worries, the ladder was in a good spot.

"No sweat, just get it done. At least by going first, you can be finished first." I thought as followed behind Jim. I knew I was getting higher up the ladder, not so much by looking down, just by the fact that the ladder bounced a little more with each step.

Within a few minutes, things started to not go so well for me. Jim was able to find the baby in the room, which I was able to easily carry down…once I was able to figure out how to get back onto the ladder from the inside of the building. I realized I placed the ladder little bit off, and while for Jim it was easy to get back out because he was taller, I had to literally throw a high roundhouse kick (thank God I knew how) to get my leg over the window ledge (which was about as high as my chest) and where I could get back onto the ladder. I climbed back up for the "second victim," which Jim was having trouble finding.

"Get in there and help him out," yelled one of my instructors who was standing just inside the window by the ladder. "Your partner can't find the other person." I got on my hands and knees and started by crawling along the wall just like we were taught to do in class. Keeping along the wall (when possible) reduces the chance of getting disoriented or lost when you can't see. My eyes strained to adjust from the bright outside to the dark inside, and the closer I got to smoke, the worse my vision became until I all I could see was black in front of me.

"Any luck Jim? Are you good?" I shouted. I kept sweeping my hands, halligan, and leg across the floor as I moved in hopes of finding the rescue dummy.

"I can't find him!" I heard his voice.

Suddenly, I hit some wooden post and reaching around a bit more, I felt Jim. I felt around the post and soon enough felt a mattress and more wood. We were both at the bed.

"The baby was on here, but I haven't found anyone else," he said. "Damn it."

For several more seconds we felt around, on the bed, under the bed, around the bed. No luck. We continued our way around the area, finding a chair and other random objects. I started to make my way back to a wall, and as I kept working my way around, my hand hit something sort of solid, but it moved pretty easily. I tried to pick it up and it kind of just flopped. I put the halligan down next to me against the wall so I wouldn't lose it, and started to feel for the object again. With relief I realized it was the dummy and the floppy part was its arm. It was propped up against the wall.

"I got him!" I immediately shouted to Jim. "I'm bringing him over." We already figured out that I would take any smaller "child or infant" dummy, and Jim was going to take the bigger rescue dummy. Even so, of course I still had to pull my weight (no pun intended), and I had the task of getting the dummy to him as he positioned himself onto the ladder to get down. While I was able to get the dummy to the window fairly easily, poor Jim had to work extra hard to get it up over the ladder in a way that he could still position him (the dummy) to carry him down. The minute I started to lift the dummy up toward Jim, my heart sank as I remembered my ladder placement and how high the bottom of the window was from the floor.

"You dumbass, you really screwed up, didn't you?" I said to myself. I was embarrassed and angry at myself. While I knew I couldn't just quit, my confidence boost from earlier flew right out the window faster than I could get myself out of the window. While we managed to complete the task, I knew I could've done better. As I walked with Jim to get water, I sensed he was a little irritated. I offered my apology and also hoped for a little encouragement.

"Thanks for pulling that extra weight," I said. "If I would've just placed that ladder a little better. I could've lifted better." Jim didn't say anything.

My confidence was shot. It was my own dumb fault. Knowing that in real life my mistake could have made a difference in helping people made me pretty disappointed. Then there was always the sense that people might blame my gender for any incompetency, and that didn't help. Even telling myself that I was still learning the skills for the first time gave me little consolation. I told myself it will get better, and just carried on the rest of the day as best as I could.

I had been training to become a volunteer firefighter for a small town in North Carolina. My time training and volunteering was short-lived. I moved to Texas when I accepted a job as a high school teacher, and unfortunately, that move had to happen right before completing my training to earn what is known as a "black helmet," the color of the firefighting helmet received once you passed the training. I was heartbroken, seeing as I had come *so* close. However, as I knew by then, life is full of twists, turns, and important decisions.

Along with the experiences and knowledge I gathered while volunteering and training, I picked up many important life lessons. One lesson was simply about not quitting. You don't quit in the middle of a mistake you realize you've made; you don't quit when you're tired; you don't quit when it feels like some people may doubt your abilities. Lastly, you don't quit when you convince yourself you don't know what you're doing, and you are simultaneously fighting off the biggest naysaying demon—*yourself.* Like practicing a wet exit, there are some situations where you quickly realize that your only option is to get through it. As I learned in the search and rescue drill, sometimes failing is the most difficult way to learn. Until you experience having your mental game shaken and having no other choice but to keep going, you'll never learn how to persevere. You will never experience the power you have within yourself, the power that is found by simply putting it in God's hands and then trusting yourself to just keep moving one step at a time when that is all you can do. As you will find out, the lesson of "one step at a time" came quite literally for me.

The Pucker Factor vs. the Disney Movie

My parents have always made it a point to never let my brother and me forget the value of hard work. Because of who I am physically (i.e. small), I've often been at a disadvantage in physical activities. However, I've also been sneaky about one advantage . . . I am fairly athletic. I'm no cross-fit coach, but I'm often quite agile, quicker than most people, I've got decent coordination, and although I'm no weightlifter, I am stronger than most people assume. To an extent, physical activity usually came pretty easy to me. Growing up always being the shortest (is that an oxymoron?), I quickly learned to use whatever physical abilities I had to my advantage. It was my only choice if I ever wanted to prove to other kids I was worthy of being picked to play a game.

I pat myself on the back, but I won't give myself ALL the credit. With firefighting most success is found through major teamwork. As a female in the field, even if no words were spoken, I could often sense when someone questioned not just my ability, but my desire to be in that field of work. It ain't easy, but I wanted to do it. So, I did it. Not as a challenge to the world, or even to myself. There was a desire to earn respect, but I did it simply because I wanted to be a firefighter. I just wanted to help people.

Now, while my size may be a factor, there is another "factor" of sorts that I came to learn about. It's called the

"Pucker Factor," (I'll refer to it as "PF") and apparently it runs on something like a scale of 1-10, 1 being the lowest. Some people may be familiar with what the PF is, but for those of you not familiar with it, I'll fill you in. My definition comes from an online source, Wiktionary. We all know how reliable the internet is, but based on what my firefighter instructors and cohorts have described, this definition seemed accurate.

Pucker Factor: The tightening to various degrees of the anal sphincter as a result of engaging in various acts of terror or daring. Often the use of a scale from 1 to 10 is applied to the term...[1]

One course I had to take while training was a ladders course. Ladders class was more physically demanding, than I expected. We learned about carrying and "throwing" (basically setting up) ladders. Fully extending a 35' ladder by myself the first time in class took me well over a couple minutes. That's definitely *not* good time for the task. Yes, it was embarrassing, but I never quit. When pulling the rope to extend it, I had to put *all* of my weight into it. I'd look up and see that I was only couple of inches away from the hooking the paws on the rung to secure it, but I threw so much of myself into one pull of the rope that my knees and hands were already touching the ground. Since the ground stopped me from the needed few inches to secure the paws, I would have to let it back down a few inches and do it again. And again. And again. Eventually I extended that sucker all the way and while I knew it was not in passing time, I knew that I *did* it. Each time afterwards, I learned how to do it better and faster.

During one of my practicals (which is a skills test), one of the tests included carrying an actual person down from a second- or third- story window. I knew it would be quite a task for me, but of course, I showed up that morning of testing because I'm not a quitter. Boy, was that tenacity tested.

Have you ever been so unsure about something that when the task is in front of you, you mentally tell yourself, "You can do it," because you know that's advice that a Disney movie would give you? Believe, don't quit. However, simultaneously you ask yourself, "What the hell am I thinking?" If Disney and Miley Cyrus taught me about the climb, firefighting taught me about the descent! There comes this point in your life where you realize you are not the daredevil you thought you were. I won't necessarily call it becoming a "scaredy cat," and just say that the idea that you are not invincible becomes more prominent. For our practical, I realized that as the task of the ladder rescue grew closer, my PF factor also grew higher. I even debated whether or not to ask to pass (as in skip) the rescue portion of the skills test. To put it bluntly, I doubted myself, especially after my previous experience with Jim.

By about 9 a.m. I was on a roll hauling and using equipment, and completing the other tasks for the test just fine. However, mentally, I was only focusing on what to tell my instructor about the rescue portion.

"Should I just be straight and say I would like to skip this portion of the test?" I groaned. *"That sounds so bad,"* I argued with myself. *"Should I just be honest and say I'd rather not risk anything? I mean, there is no shame in being honest with something like that, right? You're a mature adult, Nicole, you know sometimes it's best to swallow your pride."* I spent so much of the morning just arguing with myself and practicing the speech I would give my instructor.

Lunch break came, and we were dog tired, drenched in sweat. We were all a little irritated that the rescue portion of the test was after lunch.

"My fat ass can't even move when I *haven't* eaten yet," someone mumbled as we all hopped in the truck to go to the Subway down the street. We had about 45 minutes to grab a bite and get back to the test.

"I know right? This is gonna suck," someone replied. "Food coma, plus heat, plus full stomach – not a great combination." The more they talked, the more I started to think that maybe skipping that second part of the test wasn't such a bad idea. I just sat quietly the entire lunchtime.

"Ok, just tell the instructor, and be done with it," I encouraged myself. *"You've done tremendous and you have nothing to be ashamed of. Just walk up to him when we get started, and just say it."* I took out a cookie from the paper bag. *"But you've also come this far, and you CAN do this. You know you can,"* I replied, now disappointed in myself for even contemplating not finishing the test. Angry and frustrated, I shoved the macadamia nut cookie in my mouth. I figured I deserved the stupid cookie being this stressed out. *"The stress will burn off those calories in no time, and maybe eating will make me shut up about everything,"* I thought taking out a second cookie.

After what felt like too short of a lunch, we found ourselves back to the testing. *"OUCH!"* I said to no one as my shin hit the stair in front of me. *"Stupid stairs!"* I grumbled. *"Why do you do this to yourself?"* I took my time walking up the pitch-black stairwell to the room where my partner would "rescue me." My shin started to throb as I walked up the steps trying harder not to hit it again. I held onto the rail as the stairwell got darker with each step further from the door. The darkness seemed to amplify the sound of my boots scraping and clunking up the stairs.

I swore I was going to tell my instructor I was not going to be a part of this rescue. And yet, here I was. It wasn't my turn to rescue yet, but I was still mad. I wanted to quit, but I couldn't stop walking. I reached the next floor and got in position. Once positioned on my partner's leg (this rescue was done with the "victim" sitting on one of your legs to be carried down), I turned myself into a pretend unconscious victim and went completely limp. My partner handled it like a pro, and we got down in no time. I gave her a sincere smile and a "Nice work!" to congratulate her. I had nothing against her and was happy to cheer her on to her black helmet.

"Ok, shorty, you're up!" said my instructor standing at the bottom of the ladder.

"You got this!" I heard someone shout. I got an approval from my partner who started to make her way to the dark stairwell so she could get to the window to be "rescued." My heart skipped a few beats. All I had to do was tell my instructor I didn't think I could do it. I took a deep breath. However, instead of talking, I grabbed the rung on the ladder, and started to climb up. I only remember that about halfway up I glanced down and saw my peers looking up at me.

"Uhhh, I guess I'm gonna do this then," I whispered to myself. I had no argument with myself whether doubtful or encouraging. I played no "movie montage" in my head. I'm pretty sure my head was completely blank at that point, but my PF factor was pretty strong. *"Here I am,"* was all I could think. I glanced up and saw an instructor in the window and my partner ready to go. If either of them was nervous about it, neither of them showed it. So I figured I shouldn't show it either. My partner was positioned on my leg, my arms went around her, and as best as I could, I grabbed onto the side rails.

"Damn Mickey Mouse gloves," I thought as the thick gloves made it tough for me to grab anything. This was going to be tough. *"All you gotta do is say the word, and this could be over. Now would kind of be the right time to do it. Your instructor is right there,"* I said, *"No, you're already here. You can do this."* Without any thinking I started moving, and the rescue carry commenced. Remember how I described timing for breaking a board in martial arts? This was the same thing. If you don't move before you start thinking again, you'll never do it. One foot stepped down to the next rung, I found my footing, and then the other foot stepped down bringing with it my partner. No problem. One step after the other. The first several, not so bad. But as we moved on, I could tell I was getting tired and my partner could tell.

"You can do this. Remember, I can't help you, I can't move myself. Just try putting your hand on the rung here," she suggested.

"Damn gloves!!" I thought as I started to get angry. "I know you can't really help, but quick just grab the rung for a second, just grab it," I told her. I knew she wasn't allowed to, but I chose safety over the test. She grabbed it, and within a second, I found a better position.

"You good up there?" my instructor below shouted. I looked down.

"Yessir," I said, "I just gotta find my grip."

"She can't climb, remember that. She's a victim that's either unconscious or just not physically capable." Since he didn't tell me I failed, I figured he either wasn't sure what just happened, or he was letting it go this one time since I kept moving.

"Yessir, I know," I said. My PF factor once again became apparent. I just needed to finish the task. *"Please don't fail me sir,"* I thought. *"Just let me finish this, please."* I could tell that I was starting to get angry and I just wanted to scream. I wasn't angry at anyone. No one was to blame. I was just starting to get frustrated. I was mad at myself for wanting to quit, but mad at myself for not wanting to quit.

"You got it?" I heard my partner again. I was worried she was starting to become a little more unsure. "Maybe just try the rung again," she suggested.

"My hands won't fit because of the gloves." We were at a point on the ladder where two rungs (steps) were in line, so it was double the size – great for me to step on, harder for me to grasp. I was just pissed off at that point. "Ok, I'm good," I stated. My partner went "unconscious" again, and I felt her complete weight start to settle back onto me.

"Nicole, your ass better just do this because you're barely halfway down the ladder." I thought to myself. *"Trying to climb back up with the weight of gear and a carrying a grown person ain't gonna happen."* I started to mentally scream at myself. As much as tried to get my mind motivated, my thinking told me to shut-up and just think calmly through it. Then, my mind told me to *stop* thinking about thinking. After that, I'm pretty sure it just told me to stop thinking. Confused about my thought process? So was I. Angry and determined, I just kept moving. My brain was throwing me every excuse in the freakin' book. I was irritated. Every time I lowered my leg, I had to brace for my partner to slide down with me.

"You had to be a firefighter didn't you, Nicole?!" there went my brain again. *"Your dumbass couldn't just stay a freakin' special education teacher, could you? What am I doing, God? I asked you to help me make a decision about my career. What is going on? Is this your way of saying I should've stayed in a classroom?"* At that second I realized that no, I couldn't stay a teacher because I wasn't happy being one, at least not at that moment in my life. *"Is this what you want then?"* I asked myself. Maybe scolding myself would help. As I slowly moved my feet and hands in rhythm, all I kept seeing was the evenings I would get home from work as a teacher, shut the door, put my things down, and break down into tears. *"Well, hell, here you are, Nicole,"* I said as I continued to move down the ladder. *"I know two things: I am NOT going back to teaching, and right now I'm*

128

stuck on a damn ladder." I took a breath. *"I can't climb back up after going this far, especially wearing all this gear and carrying someone. I can't just quit and put her back in the window!"* And then, it clicked.

If I played my cards right, then everything that was working against me in the task at hand, was also working *with* me. As I tried to fight off the realization that my little muscles were starting to burn, I remembered that my objective was to bring the victim *down* not up.

"Of course, you idiot! Just secure her and brace. Why they heck are you trying to lift her? You're going down, not up. And thank goodness you're small yourself, that's less weight to carry. Let the gravity help you, just keep moving. I don't know what the hell I'm doing with my life right now, but I do know I'm going to get down from here and finish this."

Step by step, step by step, was what I needed. As each step started to get smoother and more in rhythm, I began to hear voices that were just a minute ago drowned out by my thoughts. It was the sound of my peers getting louder and clearer.

"You're almost there, girl, keep on coming!" I heard. I looked down to see how far I actually had to go. I had been so busy arguing with myself that I never bothered to check. I still had a ways to go, but I laughed as I realized it. My boys were cheering me on. I started to enjoy what I was doing. I was unsure about so much at that moment in my life, but overall, I knew I was going to be just fine. A little well-deserved pride for not quitting just moments ago began to grow inside me. Each step down felt more in rhythm, and in the midst of what felt like an endless mental and physical battle, I suddenly heard my partner.

"You can let go of me now," she said laughing. I snapped back to reality.

"Huh?" I was confused.

She laughed. "My feet are on the ground." I looked down and realized another advantage to my height. While I was still trying to climb down three rungs, she was already standing on the ground.

"Oohhhh! My bad," I said as we both started laughing. So, in the midst of it all I learned that sometimes you just have to do it. No matter what your brain is telling you in the middle of the chaos, sometimes you have to trust your training, trust God, and just GO. Just like capsizing, you're in the middle of it whether you like it or not, and there is no turning back.

So, what was my fear all morning? What was the cause for my PF to climb? I cannot really tell you because I *truly* cannot pick out any one major factor. Was it the pressure of having a real person depending on me to get her to safety? Was it the possibility of failing the test? Was it knowing that sometimes people might doubt my ability? Maybe it was a combination of everything. Maybe all of it made me doubt my decision in career changes, and that in turn made me doubt my entire reason for trying to be a firefighter. Maybe thinking of teaching made teaching a comfort zone for a moment in time while I clung to the ladder. I really don't know. But we all know comfort zones can hold you back.

To my rescue partner at the time, shout out to you! She is an awesome person, and I am happy to say that today she also happens to be a certified firefighter! Thanks for trusting me, or at least pretending to! That went a long way. And a shout out to all my guys who helped and supported me through each task!

I can't help but smile when I think back to the stories and memories of training. I'm sad I never got to complete the training after getting so far. However, sometimes that's how it goes. After moving away, I taught high school math for one more year, and decided again to give a career as a first responder another shot. I took the paramedic route, and while I completed the program, I worked as an EMT for only a little less than two years.

Although this PF thing has an obvious presence in something like rescuing a person, I have found that much of what we do in life will involve a pucker factor. Taking risks and making changes always involves some degree of doubt and fear. When you're in it deeply, you get to that point that I mentioned earlier. You think to yourself, "You can do this, just keep going," and at the same time you ask yourself, "What the hell am I doing?" Well, here are some things I've learned. Every person's situation brings unique factors to the table (including the PF). Regardless of that, I hope some of these little lessons of mine will be helpful to you in some way.

First, it really is about perspective. The weight of your stress might linger, but if you play your cards right, that weight can become your saving grace. I suppose my rescue training is a bit more of a literal example, but carrying a person who was bigger than me could have easily made me focus on how unfair things *appeared* to be. But it was not unfair. It was reality. I am small. If I wanted to be a firefighter, I can't use that as an excuse. Sometimes you can take an obstacle and blow it up in front of your face, so it is all you see. In my case, the goal was to rescue my partner, period. I had to carry a person DOWN, and it's not like she was stopping me from going down. Yes, carrying someone added to the stress, but that contributing factor was also going in the same direction I was going, not against me.

Secondly, pride makes you fight for the wrong things and makes you miss out on the REAL gift . . . living life and having chances to help others. Again, my goal during the skills test was to help my partner. It did not matter if the entire class watched me and was impressed, or if the only witness was the person

I was trying to help. It was not about putting on a show. It was about trying to do something good, about willingly giving everything I had towards accomplishing something positive for the greater good.

To help swallow your pride you must focus on the true reason you do something, and if that reason is selfish, you better fix that quick. Do you know what a priest once told me in confession? I had talked to him about my struggle with pride and getting it mixed in with my decisions about where I was going with my life. He looked right at me and smiled. At this confession, the priest and I sat across from each other, no screen was in between this time.

"No one cares," he said. I stared back at the priest, completely caught off guard.

"Uhhhh," I said. I thought the burping priest was one for the ages, but *this* dude! He gently said it again.

"No one really cares what you do with your life." Imagine a priest telling you that when you expect consolation! I remember just sitting there blankly staring at him and trying to figure out this "game" he was playing with my head.

"Wait, this is a church right?" I thought to myself. I looked to my left to make sure that was actually a crucifix with Jesus on the wall. I looked at the priest again, and he was still smiling. I shifted in my seat. I desperately tried to

make sense of what he said and before I started to panic, it suddenly, clicked. It made all the difference in the world and I felt my muscles relax and my frown go away. *"I am so glad I went to confession."* I thought as I felt a small smile turn up the corner of my mouth. The priest continued. I could tell he realized it made sense to me now.

"Ultimately, no cares what you do as far as a career. It's not because people don't care about *you*, but as far as careers go, let's face it, everyone is busy with their own well-being too. Follow where the Holy Spirit steers you."

It makes sense. Don't waste time trying to meet expectations or worrying if people agree with you. Listen to their input, but don't let *them* make your decisions *for* you. In the end, are *you* happy with how you're living your life? Are you living for God rather than your own recognition? Because in the end, it comes down to you and God, not the people you impressed or disappointed in your lifetime. Keep your intentions straight.

Next lesson: You'll be damned if you do, and damned if you don't. In a career where you rescue people, it's ironic that being in the position to rescue people is an initial fear. When you are new to the career, you are more than eager for that first big rescue, but you might also worry about making a mistake. It hits different when you are kneeling over a real human being who is unresponsive. Don't get me wrong, it's a legit fear. I don't believe anyone wants to be responsible for someone else's death. However, when you are trying to save a life, and you get to a point where you must do *something*, or you have to make decisions, you might just freak out. What if you mess up? Well, one of my paramedic classmates said it perfectly: If you don't try *something* at that moment, then that person you're sent to help can die anyway. This goes back to my great fear of the feeling of regret. I prefer to try my best to go to bed each night knowing, at the very least, that I tried my best that day, whatever tasks I faced. God ultimately calls the shots when it's time for someone to go home, but he uses my hands to do whatever he needs me to do whenever he needs me to do it.

Oddly enough, you also come to realize that sometimes the life you impact isn't even the one you're trying to save or help. In the midst of whatever your job is, sometimes it only takes one small encounter with someone else to keep your heart and pride in check.

One example came when I looked up to close the back of the ambulance door and saw a boy crying as he watched us take his little cousin into the ambulance, the little cousin who just minutes ago, he was playing with and pushed just a bit too hard on the swing causing an accident. Now she was going to the hospital. I could tell he felt horrible.

Another example came as a volunteer firefighter in training. It happened during Fire Safety Day at the farmers market, when one little girl came to visit me inside the truck. My heart melted as a mother looked at me and I heard her shout out to her child.

"Look, sweetie, it's a lady firefighter!" I smiled as a little face poked her head around the giant door of the truck and I helped her climb her way up to where I was standing. She pushed some hair out of her face, and mesmerized, she looked around touching the gear and the headset.

"I always wanted to be a firefighter!" she said to me excitedly. "But I never thought I could since I was a girl. Now I see that I can do it too!" I just wanted to hug this little girl. She made my day!

"Well," I said, "you can be anything you want to be! And hey!" I laughed, "I'm more than three times your age, and you're as big as me, so if I can do it, so can you! You just gotta work hard and not quit."

"That's right!" her mom chimed in behind me. "She loves fire trucks," she smiled taking pictures of her daughter with her phone.

"Yup!" the girl said smiling ear to ear. All of a sudden my sadness about leaving firefighting left me, and I felt like my entire short career as a volunteer firefighter was complete. If my biggest impact was to inspire people rather than pull them out of burning buildings, I was ok with that too.

Finally, as a teacher, I found my impact when I think about the dad of an unborn baby, the dad who also happened to be my student. He would come to my class during lunch to take a nap because it was the only time he got to sleep. He worked hard trying to make sure he would be able to provide when his child was born. I think maybe some days he inspired me more than I did him. I always wonder how he is doing these days.

So this brings me to one last thing I really love to ponder, especially with the madness that goes on in the world, the madness that each of us knows is just not right – call it racism, call it sexism, call it violence or *whatever* you want. Think about this: No matter how much we take precautions - these days wear masks, lock our doors, teach kids safety and morals, . . . No matter how paranoid people or the media can make us, it's *amazing* how human beings will put their trust in you. That is a BEAUTIFUL THING that I consider a gift from God, almost an ever-present doorway to hope. It is an opportunity to help and inspire others, *no matter* what you do. God fixes a way into *everything* you do, and sometimes in ways you least expect it. You just need to keep your eyes open to those opportunities and never take for granted even the tiniest ones. Humans, in some twisted way *do* trust each other. Even with how absolutely insane the world can show itself to be, there is a deep beauty in us inspired by fear. No one wants to hurt. I think most of the anger people feel comes from frustration of the fact that the bad things in the world are just as obvious as the most fundamental good things in the world, like kindness and a feeling of belonging. Unfortunately, we just can't agree on how to get to the good things. It's kind of ironic. That is why I turn to God, because sometimes when you're shaken enough, you can't even trust your own judgement no matter how hard you try, or how good your intentions. Sometimes the harder you push yourself to clear up your own thoughts, the more jumbled they become.

Here on earth where we do our own thing, we humans are the Lord's hands and feet, and *we* are all we have to depend on. Somehow, deep down, we know that. When sudden tragedy hits, no one stops to think of who to find for help. We *just do it.* Maybe we frantically call a neighbor, call 911, or wave down a complete stranger. And thank God that when tragedy strikes people can still surprise us with a helping hand or encouraging act.

Anytime we reach that Pucker Factor of 10, remember that you must keep the factors themselves in perspective, swallow your pride so that you *can* keep your priorities in perspective, and never forget that even amongst the naysayers, we need to work together and support each other. Believe in yourself. Sometimes that means that when you doubt the most or when your world capsizes, trust God's plan, and just face the task in front of you.

7

SEASONS

♪

As I waited in my car for the lady to open the sliding window so I could pay for my food, I was a bit frantic. "Don't cry, don't cry," I whispered to myself as I swallowed a lump in my throat. "Hold on. Just make it home first." I started to shake my leg, like I do sometimes when I'm anxious. Frantically, I searched for my friend's phone number on my phone so I could talk to her. That always helps me when I'm upset. As I fumbled through the screen on my phone I didn't realize that the cashier had opened the sliding window and was waiting on me.

"Oh sorry," I blurted out, panicking to get my money. I fumbled through my wallet and my debit card was so snug in the pocket that I had trouble sliding it out.

"*No no no, come on,*" I thought. "*Just get your stupid sandwich and get out of here.*" I was about to burst into tears as I tried so hard to push back down the lump that reappeared in my throat. I knew my eyes were getting watery. I knew the cashier was waiting for me. "*I knew I should've just gone straight home.*" You see, I am a stress eater, and that day driving home from class, I didn't have to think twice to pull straight into the drive-thru on my way home.

As I started to pull out the card and hand it to the cashier, I heard the cashier mumble into her headset, "Mmm hmm, this customer here wasn't paying attention, too busy on her phone."

That was all it took, the straw that broke the camel's back. Out of nowhere I burst into a serious set of tears. The cashier was right, but all I wanted was a friend to talk to, and that's all I was trying to find on the phone. The lady taking my money apologized, realizing I was upset.

"Don't worry about it," I mumbled. Then I grabbed my receipt and drove up to the next window. As I pulled up to the next window and looked up to get my food, the lady handing me my food helplessly asked if I was ok. There was no hiding it now. I sat there sniffing back snot, and wiping tears out of my eyes, my voice cracking as I tried to say I was ok. I was a glob of embarrassment and frustration. I was hungry, and at the same time wanted to throw away the bag of food that was just handed to me. I just wanted to get home so I could cry in private. I folded up the top of the paper bag to close it, said thanks, and drove off.

At the traffic light, a panhandler began to approach me. I looked up at his dirty hat and flannel shirt. We made eye contact, and when he saw me choking on tears, he bowed his head, turned around, and walked back to his overturned crate to sit down. At that point I *knew* that the look on my face must have been pretty miserable. I kind of hoped he came to my window anyway so we could chat while I waited at the light. I didn't need to talk about my problems. I just wanted a friend right then. I kind of wanted to hug him and thought we could *both* use a hug.

I was tired, but it was not sleep I needed. I was tired of school, work, and feeling like I was getting nowhere. In all reality, with the age I was at and all of the schooling I had already completed, I could have had a Ph.D. by then. The spinning world made me dizzy, or was that my throbbing head and stuffy nose from crying? All I needed was for everything to just work out, even though I knew it wouldn't happen in a day. If only I could snap my fingers and wake up to an awesome steady job and no more schoolwork. The most frustrating thought was that I couldn't do *anything* to speed up the days in front of me. My only option was to continue, day by day, class after class, work hour after work hour . . . not the most encouraging thought at a time like that.

Amazingly, my friend called me right in the middle of this little episode. Coincidence? I think not. I sat at the traffic light and sobbed away.

"Hang in there, Nic," she told me. "This is just a season. It will be over."

* * *

I suppose that it can be difficult to end a lot of things, whether you're ending a book, winding down the weekend, or nearing the end of a career. Perhaps the hard part is actually figuring out *how* to end it. There are so many factors to weigh. For example, there may be loved ones involved in your decisions, or maybe a financial risk. Maybe, you simply *don't want* something to end. It's all about perspective, remember? Face it - time drags on when something sucks . . . but time flies when you're having fun. Either way, no matter what kind of day you are having, 24 hours in a day is *always* 24 hours in a day. No more, no less, nothing else.

Well, the day after my drive-thru breakdown, I thought about it. A season. It sounded way more poetic and encouraging to look at my situation as a "season" as opposed to something more defined, like hours or, in my case, the number of semesters remaining before I can earn a certification, or, even the number of years it might take to finally settle comfortably into a career. Can I be honest? I was grateful for the jobs I had because I needed them. However, I didn't want the jobs I had. In my heart of hearts I just *knew* I could be more. I told myself countless times to stop whining and remember that I am blessed to have even one job.

At that moment, I made a couple of mental notes. First, never make stressful moments in your life a countdown to something better. I began to notice that I only started to see numbers of a countdown and miss out on everything else. Secondly, I reminded myself of my "coffee-induced revelation," that no one's life is perfect. I needed stop comparing who I am and where I am in life to everyone I see. Taking joy in someone else's *worse* situation is awful, and taking for granted what you have because of someone's *better* situation is awful. Just keep moving forward. At some point you realize that moving forward might be the only positive thing you *can* do, just like in capsizing and fighting that "PF," it is a matter of appreciating where God has placed you and *focusing on the task at hand.* I'm working for God's glory and to get to Heaven. Focus on that. Taking the perspective of "seasons" is a bit more productive, than countdowns and comparisons. Similar to moments in life, seasons are inevitable. No matter the order, duration, or characteristics of the seasons, each brings a necessity for our lives to be complete.

There is a song from the late 1950's/early 1960's sung by The Byrds called "Turn Turn Turn." The words reference a portion of the book of Ecclesiastes in the Bible. Some examples from the Bible are:

"There is an appointed time for everything, and a time for every affair under the heavens.

A time to give birth, and a time to die...

A time tear down, and a time to build...

A time to mourn, and a time to dance...

A time to rend, and a time to sew..." [1]

The song lyrics are fairly accurate to the book, and both help a person recognize the value of moments in our lives. However, it always helps to read a little before and a little after a selected verse or chapter in the Bible for more context. The song references the beginning of a chapter in the book. If you were to read the book a bit beyond the song lyrics to "Turn Turn Turn," it goes on to say, *"I recognized that there is nothing better than to rejoice and to do well during life,"* [2] which brings me back to making the effort to appreciate where you are in life and the importance of focusing on the task at hand.

Life is full of experiences. Sometimes many people are a part of your experience, and other times you must face uncertainty all by yourself. Let me remind you I'm not nearly old enough to call myself wise, yet I'm confident enough to say that I've been through a good number of circumstances to have become a little more knowledgeable with each step. While some experiences made me question my confidence and competence, they have none the less proven to me how much stronger and tougher I am, especially with God on my side. They remind me that God is the prime example of a friend – *always* there, 24-7. Even more, God only ever wants what is best. Now THAT's a friend who loves you. He is so committed, that God will not hesitate to hurt your feelings if it means it will bring you to something greater than your own desires. Don't you appreciate honesty in a friend, even if it sometimes hurts? If you choose to listen, it only helps you become better.

8

A Little Faith in a Not So Little God: The Crazy Easter Egg Hunt

☙

In case you haven't picked up on it, God is a constant for me. While writing about my experiences, it never failed that I came across a moment where I had to give credit to God for being with me in some way. For example, I am blessed and thankful for supportive family and friends. However, in the times that even they couldn't help me anymore than they already did, who did I always turn to? God. He has yet to fail me. I bring this up to point out that when I look back to moments I felt the most lonely, the most consistent and comforting realization is that I know that my God lives. He is always present, and well, thank God for that! Now, my intention here is not to shove my faith in anyone's face, and by no means am I calling any human being less than me if they are wary about their belief in Christ. My hope is to merely encourage any person who is willing and open-minded enough to read what I have written.

Washed by the Water, to Get Thrown in the Dirt

I believe there is a difference between sharing your faith and showing off your faith. Whether you choose to believe in God is completely *your* choice. In fact, as I thought about it, I came to the conclusion that if God and Satan have anything in common, it is that they ultimately give *you* the choice to pick the direction you want to go. I think that in the process of sharing and living your faith, you inevitably *show* your faith. I challenge you to make the effort to take a situation, see it as an opportunity, and carefully make choices. Along with that you must also come to terms with the realization that in the most unpleasant situations, seeing opportunity requires an extra effort. The inventor Thomas Edison said, "*Opportunity is missed by most people because it is dressed in overalls and looks like work."* Well, literally for God's sake, get your hands dirty.

C.S. Lewis wrote a book entitled *Mere Christianity*, where he states, *"...that is [just] why a vague religion – all about feeling God...is so attractive. It is all thrills and no work."*[1] Like I learned about stepping outside the church walls, the world you must face is *outside* of the walls and there is always work to be done. As a Catholic, I take seriously my practice and that is part of the work. For example, as described in an early chapter, practicing the sacrament of reconciliation (confession), is not a gift made for convenience. It is meant to give grace to try again to be a better person than you were the day before. In doing so you face challenges and temptation. You have to *work* to be a better you, be it a better sibling, parent, friend, or Christian.

It seems that a true journey to Heaven is not just a stroll through the park. When your only way out is through, then charge ahead without second thought. And if you are doing it right, then hopefully one day you will step back from your efforts, take a breath, peek behind you, and quietly say, "Well I'll be darned, look how far I've come! Thank you, God." You might surprise yourself at how far you've made it. And when the world catches up, turn forward, take a deep breath, and keep on running. You may not necessarily see ahead, but you know where you are headed anyway. And isn't that kind of the definition of faith? Not to physically see or feel what you are going after, but rather to believe that it *is* there.

When you are so low that you don't *feel* like you believe in anything anymore, that is when you must *keep telling yourself* you believe. The results will come if you stay true to the race you run. I will warn you though, do not allow that race to be solely against anyone or anything. Rather, let it be a race to get to where you want to go. For me, that goal is Heaven. If you get distracted, then your race only becomes longer and your heart loses focus. This often results in what we usually call a heartbreak. You allow influences like pride, impatience, or anger, to make you vulnerable to the wrong goals. One of, if not my favorite Bible chapter is Hebrews chapter 12, where it says:

> . . . *let us rid ourselves of every burden and sin that clings to us and persevere in running the race that lies before us while keeping our eyes fixed on Jesus...For the sake of the joy that lay before him he endured the cross...opposition from sinners, in order that you may not grow weary and lose heart...Endure your trials as "discipline"...discipline seems a cause not for joy...yet later it brings the peaceful fruit of righteousness to those who are trained by it. So strengthen your drooping hands and your weak knees. Make straight paths for your feet, that what is lame may not be dislocated but healed.* [2]

Do not quit fighting the good fight, no matter what your circumstances. And try not to complain to Jesus about how life isn't fair. Just remember that Jesus himself dealt with backstabbing, mocking, arguments, heartbreak, fear, opposition to his standards and beliefs, and physical and emotional pain. So, *who are we* to whine about these things? Instead, persevere trusting in God. Jesus rose from the dead, but *only after* turning his life over to God's will and allowing himself to die.

More often than I deserve, opportunities present themselves. Yes - *more* than I would like. How so? Once again, it's all about perspective. First of all, if you ever find yourself in a situation that is tough because of the fact that you *have* options, contemplate the idea that maybe you should be thankful that the obstacle you face is having to *actually* choose. Sometimes having options *is* the opportunity, and it may be more than what other people might have. Even if it's a difficult decision, it quite possibly comes with at least a couple of valuable consequences and opportunities:

1) Tough decision-making is where life's greatest lessons are often rooted.

2) Facing "adulting" (i.e., having responsibilities, accepting consequences) makes you remember to appreciate simple things like a moment of peace early

in morning, or the random discovery of a $5 bill in your jacket pocket.

3) Tough decisions = analyzing pros/cons, which can also lead to discovering or re-discovering blessings!

4) Tough decisions indicate that you have the chance to quite possibly move forward. That, my friend, is something of TREMENDOUS value when your days are filled with wondering if anything you do is of worth. With time, you discover that even what seems to have been a waste of time has value in your journey. So long as every step you take has the purpose of moving forward, then it is always worth something. If your life were a story, the "meat of it" comes in the middle, not the beginning . . . and surprisingly, not the end.

Marinating the Meat in the Middle

Let me start with revisiting something I mentioned a while back. I have accomplished not much of what I "planned" to set out and do. Several years is a good chunk of my time and a good chunk of my youthful enthusiasm. However, several years is not a lot in the grand picture. Obviously, there have been many moments of discouragement or frustration. Despite these things, in my HEART of HEARTS, and food-loving gut of mine, I feel like a new season is coming.

I have become more aware of who I am and the type of lifestyle I want to have. Jumping into a new career can be an exciting adventure. However, when you do it numerous times and always give it everything you have got, then each new start becomes filled with a little less excitement and little more anxiety. When it felt like I was going in circles on a runway and everyone else in the world was flying by me, my faith in my own decisions became wary. But, my faith in God only grew stronger. The good Lord is working back there, up there, around here, SOMEWHERE, and in the meantime, I must continue press on. The meat in the middle of my life is marinating, and if I want flavor in the meat, then I need patience in the wait! These circumstances are God's teaching tools, his grace, and my opportunities. People, things, and time, come and go. Isn't that a gift?

As a kid thinking about a career, I said I would never work with kids, but I discovered new passions and courage becoming a teacher. Looking further down the road, when did I *ever* envision myself as a firefighter or working on an ambulance? Never. The training I have done, the strength I have found, the realization of the heroine I *really* wanted to be, are priceless lessons. It has nothing to do with running into the burning building and everything to do with not quitting and being a role model for little girls who told me they didn't believe they could be a firefighter. Hopefully I was a role model for anyone who doubted his or her chances or abilities in life. I was given a gift to be an example of hope for them, so long as I was willing to face the challenges that came with finding the gift.

The Crazy Easter Egg Hunt

What is the purpose of life? While I cannot objectively provide an answer to the purpose of life that is tailored to your (the reader's) specific situation, I can share my thoughts. If God wakes me up each day with some degree of ability, then he *must* keep me around for the sole reason that I still have work to do. As a Catholic, I was taught that my purpose includes knowing and loving God,[3] as well as serving God. During my mother's final days in home hospice, I began to learn and see how my mom's words and life provided many examples of a good Christian. Her dying also helped me begin to understand what it meant whenever someone would say that God determines when I am done, simply because God decided I was worthy enough to put on this Earth.

We come into this world. We do stuff. We die. So, what's the point? Maybe this isn't a new concept, but here's a little bit of what I think. Life is not about finding your purpose. Life is about LIVING your purpose. I think it is ironic and irritatingly funny that the process of "finding your purpose" kind of *is* living your purpose. That's twisted, almost cruel, and yet . . . beautifully complex. Through these tremendously difficult (yet blessed) years that have passed, and including where I currently am in life, so much *stuff* has happened. While I may get into moods of moping around wondering if I'll ever get anywhere, one revelation always keeps me going: No matter how discouraged I get, how physically, mentally, even spiritually tired I get, I have never looked back. I do not regret a single step or shift I have made in my life, whether the road was rocky or not.

As far as direction in my life, I admit I often feel lost, but I truly believe that I am *not* lost. I said numerous times that regret is my greatest fear. I try to use that to guide my decisions. More importantly, I try to keep my focus on God. In every scary decision I've made, the last thing I say before that big leap of faith is always along the lines of this speech:

"Ok. Focus on God's will. I will put my life in your (God's) hands. It's you (God) and me because you're all I've got . . . and that's not a bad thing. I don't know what the hell I'm doing, but I trust in you, Lord." An awkward prayer, but an *honest* one. If all I had left in this world was myself and the presence of God, I think I'd be ok. In fact, that scenario might even be perfect – just my most trusted friend, and me.

To find your purpose, you must LIVE your purpose. God hides all these opportunities like some crazy Easter egg hunt. Have you ever watched kids on an Easter egg hunt? Have you ever noticed how the older the group of children, the "harder the level" the adults make the hunt? When the kids are really little, the eggs are EVERYWHERE just scattered on the open grass, and the opportunities are endless! The hardest part as a child is being able to grab everything before your eyes! When you watch as an adult, you laugh and smile at the kids who are so overwhelmed at everything around them. At this point, they joyfully run around and there are practically no obstacles. Those adorable little hands and feet happily scramble around to collect eggs. Some pick up one egg and spend forever just trying to open it to see what is inside. As the eggs all around them are slowly taken by others, the child opening his or her *one* egg doesn't seem to care. Parents frantically direct their child.

"Put it in your basket, we'll open it later, go get some more!" followed by a gentle push or tug to get the child moving. But the child is determined just to see what one egg holds. What a gift it is to be able to have so much excitement over one simple chance.

As kids get older, the game changes—the eggs become harder to find, the other kids become tougher (and smarter) competitors, and worst of all, kids become old enough to realize that some eggs have "good prizes," while other eggs don't. And admit it, we all know in the back of everyone's mind is the desire to figure out where that egg holding the money is located. I know I was. Heck, I'm still always watching the kids to see who finds it. That's life, ain't it?

Isn't it ironic that the two biggest holidays that celebrate Jesus are also the two seasons that tug the hardest at the basic, yet essential moral lessons? It's not about gifts. It's not about eggs with prizes. It's about love. Now, don't get me wrong, I think it's ok to give everyone, young and old, something to enjoy. It's fun! As long as we make it a point to never lose focus. Speaking of which, back to it . . .

As I've been wandering down this road of mine, this "Easter Egg Hunt," if you will, of trying to find a career, there's a part of me that tries to plan things out accordingly, and a part of me that makes an effort to make sure I remember the importance of doing something I will be *happy* doing. I *want* to find that good egg. Other days it feels like I *need* that egg. But do I?

"Living your purpose," is kind of like your Easter egg hunt. God has laid out all these eggs for you and gives you the free will to make your choices. Every person's path is different. However, each path is an opportunity, and some eggs will have prizes you get excited about, some will be less exciting, but a prize is there regardless. As you get older, you become more cautious about which egg you choose and the people or obstacles you encounter to get to that egg. I'd like to share a few "eggs" that have popped up along my hunt.

They were "money eggs," but they also contained a little more than that. They were also quite literally handed to me in the midst of my decisions to choose other eggs.

9

THE ANDREW JACKSON CHALLENGE

ॐ

Well Played, God, Well Played

After leaving the teaching profession (the first time), I found myself training and taking classes to become a firefighter. To help financially, I worked part time a couple days a week as a tutor, which freed up many mornings. I often went to a café or coffee shop where I studied and used the time to begin writing this book. One hot summer day, I was driving home from the park after a jog, and I stopped by an ATM to get $20. Mom always taught me to have at least a little cash in my pocket, (great advice by the way) just in case, so I made the pit stop.

As I withdrew the money, that all-too-familiar wave of self-pity started to flow over me. I knew I was not poor; I knew I would be ok. However, every time I withdrew money, it made me realize that with a part-time tutoring job, the money going into my account would never catch up with the money going out. My mother used to also say, "It's not how much money you put in, it's how much money you put out." More good advice. I looked down at my $20 bill and thought, *"Well, this sucks."* I sighed and told myself, "This firefighting and all, it's gonna be worth it. Just hang in there." I worked hard to push away the bad feeling lurking within. I folded up the bill and moved on. I got into Nunny (my car), threw the bill onto the little console under the radio, and drove toward home. Making a right out of the parking lot, I knew that there was a Starbucks on the way.

"Hmmmm, maybe I'll do a little writing and get a drink," I thought. Then my mind started to argue with itself. I thought of the $20 I *just* withdrew. I drove down Battleground Avenue and braced myself for the hissy-fit that I knew was about to flood my mind.

"What the hell am I doing? For crying out loud, Nicole, make the $20 bucks last more than 10 minutes! Don't spend

money on drinks you don't even really like that much…" That other voice chimed in. *"But you don't spend much, so it's ok to take a moment for myself, right?"*

I made it to a red light and stopped. Turning right would move me along toward home, but it also brought me to the entrance of Starbucks. Since it was a right turn, I could have gone if it was clear, but instead I sat there contemplating going home or stopping for a treat. It felt like such a drastic decision. Little did I know that my decisions that day would have a profound impact on my outlook of my life at the moment, and even in the future.

"Screw it," I said. "I'm going to Starbucks. Maybe I'll just get a bottle of water." As if that would make me feel better about my decision. "It's not like I go get my nails done and buy new clothes every week," I blabbered on to make myself feel better. As I rounded the corner, I saw the panhandler who was always at that same corner. I looked at my $20 bill, and became irritated, almost angry. I had made my decision, but now I was just mad. I groaned and whined.

"I know it could be way worse." I quietly said. "Thank you, God, for being so patient with me. I'm sorry when I take things for granted. Please know that I AM thankful. But please know that I'm still frustrated. No matter how scared I am to spend money, you still give me enough to waste at a Starbucks." I paused. "I'm such an idiot."

What a weird prayer. What a stupid argument with myself. I sat there and sighed staring at Andrew Jackson on that beloved $20 bill. It all seemed so simple. Just don't go to Starbucks. How is it that such a decision seemed to hold so much weight?

I knew I should give something to that guy on the corner because no matter how tough my situation was, I could still eat out. Through God's grace, I never did not have enough. Something wasn't right in my gut. Even more irritated, I went inside, spent a little time writing and purchased a drink. I convinced myself that I will do better . . .whatever THAT meant.

About 30 minutes passed, I finished up, and began heading toward my car. That nagging anger mixed with guilt followed me like the dirt around Pigpen from the *Peanuts* cartoon. Once again, I said screw it.

"If I can get a stupid mocha, I can get this dude a bottle of water." So, I pouted my way back into Starbucks and I bought a bottle of water. I went to my car, put my backpack in the trunk, took a moment to stare at my bunker (firefighter) gear sitting there, and sighed. "*Is* it going to be worth it?" I was thinking about finishing my firefighting training. "What am I doing with my life? My situation?" I groaned, wadded up a $5 bill from my change, shoved it in my pocket, and shut the trunk. Still irritated, I started talking to myself again.

I'm convinced that God makes you have frustrating conversations with yourself when he's about to blow your mind.

"Go do right, Nicole. Even if you want to hang onto your grudge and your money, go say hi to this guy, with your best effort. Do it simply because you are blessed." I tried to ease my own mind. After all, no one else would ease my mind. "As much as you blow money on coffee shops, you haven't ended up asking for money with a cardboard sign. Someone is having extra mercy on you!"

I walked over, poked my head around the big electrical box, and found the man sitting there in the shade of the pine trees, dirty ball cap on his head, faded clothes, and a scruffy beard. A dirty red backpack sat at his feet. I automatically started to feel more cheery and friendly, the kind of friendly I hadn't felt in a long time.

"Hey, sir, I brought you some water." He immediately looked over and stood up. *"Oh man,"* I thought holding out the bottle and money, *"please don't be creepy or dangerous."*

"Oh, well thank you so much," he replied with a confident and genuinely appreciative tone. He walked toward me, took the bottle and money, put the sign under his arm, opened the bottle, and took a sip.

"Say something," I thought and started to panic. There was an awkward silence, and I didn't want to just say bye and leave. So, putting aside all "stranger danger" fear I blurted.

"My name's Nicole." I extended my hand thinking, *"Hmm, probably shouldn't give my name out. Oops."* I smiled. He smiled back and shook my hand.

"Hello, Nicole, my name is Al." The rest is history.

I made a pretty cool friend. We talked for about 15 minutes or so, and while I wanted to encourage him, he ended up taking the words from me and telling me everything I needed to hear! As he told me bits and pieces about himself and his story, he told me, "God is good, you gotta have faith, you know?"

"Yessir," I said. He just continued with his stories.

"…and I made mistakes, but you know, you just gotta make choices in life, just make sure they're good ones. I made some bad ones, and it's too late now. But here I am, you know?"

"Yessir," I said. He shared so much, that I think my name was almost the extent of what I had told him about myself. I admit that at moments I had to hold back tears, tough it out, and keep talking. I gave him only some of what I had left of the $20 I'd withdrawn less than an hour ago. What a shame that I still spent more money on myself.

"Nicole," I kept telling myself, *"you just smile and share that smile with this guy! He needs it. Don't you cry, Nicole."* As much as I kept looking him in the eyes confidently during conversation, I know I also looked down plenty of times, drawing in the dirt with the tip of my shoe or kicking at the roots of the tree. *"Don't you cry."* Through every "yessir," I managed to choke out, I kept thinking, this was backwards. I'm supposed to be helping *him* today, not the other way around! I felt uncomfortable... but not in a bad way. The conversation came down to three lessons: have faith, make good choices, don't give up.

The conversation slowed down, and I said I had to run. Saying goodbye, I held back tears as I smiled, shook his hand, and made my way back to my car. Driving home, I soon found that the road got a little blurry, and with each blink of my eyes, it cleared as tears slid down my cheeks.

"Well played, God," I thought as I sniffled. *"Well played."*

The Lord works in mysterious ways, and I have learned that if you give of yourself with the right intention (even if you're fighting yourself to stop holding a grudge), some amazing things happen. God didn't answer my previous griping, angry prayers, and hissy-fit by striking me down. Instead, he answered me through some gentle acts of kindness. The catch was that I had to swallow my pride and anger and do something kind for someone else. So simple, so powerful. I feel like only through me trying to grit my teeth and remember how much I *do* have, could God have done what he did. There is your example of an opportunity, a chance to make someone's day. All it took was a willingness to say hi.

After that day, I would stop by at least once a week and chat with my new friend. I heard about his job painting buildings in Florida and stories about his ex-wife, stories about how he used railroad tracks to improve his footwork as a professional boxer, and stories about his love for old country music.

Christmastime came around, and I decided to get Al a nice card and put $20 inside. I made sure the card included mentioning Jesus because Al's biggest impact on me was his sharing of his faith in our talks. It was a simple card, and the front had a glittery angel holding a trumpet. When I went to drop it off, Al wasn't there. I figured it was a bit too cold outside and he was just somewhere inside that day. I tried a few more times that week, but I never saw him...ever again. It made me sad. It was like I *needed* our conversations, and I missed my friend. Maybe he was the angel sent to keep me on track and his job was done. Maybe he was a human who moved along on his way. I never spent that $20, and in fact I keep it sealed inside the same Christmas card and envelope. As you'll see in the next story, tucking away $20 was almost becoming a trend that started from the previous Christmas. Every time I see that envelope, there is a tiny wave of sadness in my heart, but I can only smile when I think of my buddy sitting underneath the shade of the pine trees on that summer day. I know that ultimately, in the end, I will see him again. Until then, I keep "Andrew Jackson" tucked away as a reminder of not only Al, but of his lessons and reminders that still help me keep life in perspective.

The Andrew Jackson Challenge

To get an idea of where "Andrew Jackson" *first* gave me a new perspective, I'll take you back to the Christmas before I moved to Texas and the Christmas before I met Al. While it's easy to remember things like the previous $16.72 amount dwindling in my bank account, I try to count blessings and remember how God provides in other ways. No matter how close I have ever cut it being low on money, no matter how many times I have had to put groceries back on the shelf in the store to make sure I wisely spent money, I *never didn't* have enough money. I have had an ironic revelation where I realized that sometimes you come across some money when you need it most, *but* you feel like it's not the most important thing in the world.

Around Christmas in 2015, I was chatting with one of my best friends from college, Marcos. We were doing the usual catching up. He asks how it's going and when I might get to visit him and his wife. My answer is the same as always.

"I really want to, but I don't have the money right now." It was a straightforward answer, no tears attached, or drama stories added.

"I understand," he replied. "So what *are* you up to these days anyway?"

"Heck if I know," I laughed, a quick laugh that was both a nervous laugh and a "it's crazy" kind of laugh. It's not my proudest reply, but it sure was honest! "I'm done with teaching here, and I'm finishing up the firefighter training. But I'm actually looking at trying this teaching job in Texas."

"Haha, holy cow, *Texas*?" he laughed. "You're gonna just move to Texas?"

"Maybe, haha." I laughed knowing it really was ridiculous at this point. "Dude, I don't even know anymore. But maybe a different state and school system will do me some good." There was honest hope in that thought. Anyway, the conversation went on as usual and we chatted about tennis, traveling, and college memories.

A few weeks later I received a Christmas card from Marcos. I was so excited to get a Christmas card! Call me an old fart, but snail mail always makes me smile! I opened it up, and along with a little note was a $20 bill. I smiled and read the Merry Christmas note, then tried to decide where to display my card for some holiday cheer. Should I just stand it up on the counter and start a display of cards, or maybe place it on the refrigerator? Then I paused, looked at the card, and then glanced at the picture of Andrew Jackson on the $20 bill. My smile faded and I just kind of stood there. I didn't really get sad. I didn't cry or get angry. I really can't describe what I felt. Everything just stopped. At that moment, I said that I could not stay this way.

"Never again will I let myself become this worried about money. I don't need to be rich, but I need to be comfortable," I gave myself one of those famous talks. "And never again will I push myself so hard to stay in a career because of pride, or to prove I am good at something. This is ridiculous. No more."

Standing there in my little studio apartment I turned to look at my desk. Scattered all over were resume copies, reference letters, and a plethora of documents for my application for the job in Texas, for that last desperate shot at a teaching career. Sticky notes marked different pages on the application and reminded me of deadlines and "to-do" items. Sticky notes made me feel organized. But Lord knows at that moment, my thoughts were everything *but* organized. All I knew was that I felt like my heart was drifting further and further from teaching in a classroom. Although I loved home and didn't care to live in Texas, I knew something wasn't right. I just couldn't quite figure out what. My family and friends always believed in me, and sadly I think I was becoming my own naysayer because job after job, nothing seemed to fit. But I wasn't about to quit at life.

My mind went back to the interview prior to becoming a volunteer firefighter. I recalled driving down the icy roads where a main street shrank into a smaller two-lane road and led me to fire station number 16. The station sat right in that area that transitions from a big city to a smaller country town, right across the road from the railroad tracks. As I sat at the long table surrounded by several firefighters and the chief, I remember being nervous and excited about what I knew seemed like a random choice of a career move. Looking at the snowman someone had built just outside the window, I smiled at the fact that someone put a firefighter helmet on top. I looked further out to the station entrance and saw the red, white, and blue American flag gently swaying in the wind. I thought about it. I wanted to do it, be a firefighter. However, I'd be lying if I said I was 100 percent sure about the change from teaching to firefighting. I couldn't put my finger on it, but for some reason "wanting" to do it did not feel like enough of a reason. Even if the motivation to do it was genuinely strong.

But now, was I motivated enough to move to Texas? To pick back up in a place I was unsure to be?

I snapped back to my present moment in my studio.

My Christmas card was in one hand and the faded $20 bill in the other hand. I promised I would work my way out of my situation. Someday I will not only be financially stable, but I will also find that good career, whether it was teaching, firefighting, or something else. Maybe down the road it'll change yet again, but I've got to get a move on. I challenged myself and said I would *never* spend that $20 gift. Thus started the "not so coincidence" $20 bill coincidence, of my next two Christmases. Instead of spending that first $20, I tacked it up right by my door at head level and said it will only ever serve as a reminder of my promise each day I walk out the door. What started out as a motivator soon became a significant reminder of the feeling I got that Christmas season. It would remind me that if I can stare at this bill every day and *not* spend it, (no matter how much my bills and my mind told me that I needed it), I am perfectly capable of learning to better appreciate what I *do* have. That includes the daily gift God gives to do so much more. To this day, I have that $20 bill and it sits in a box, the same box that has the Christmas card and $20 I had intended to give Al. Third time is a charm, right?...

Two years later (about six months ago from the moment I sit and draft this very chapter) "Mr. Andrew Jackson" made another important appearance in my life. He sure likes to show up when my worry about my future or my finances are on the verge of breaking me down.

Oh for the Love of God!...No, Really

First Things First

I don't want to go into detail for the sake of staying on topic. However, it is necessary to paint a picture of a situation for you. Let me start with explaining one of the toughest lessons I've had to learn in my journey thus far: some people are just mean. And while you make every effort to find good in this world and give the benefit of the doubt, while you know deep down 99 percent of people have some reason (but not necessarily an excuse) to be bitter, you finally admit—sometimes people really can be mean.

No matter what field I pick for my career, I strive to hold onto my values and whatever my motivation for choosing a career might be. I found two recurring goals: to help people and to share my gifts with others. Experience proves that there is as much variation in *how* I strive for these goals, as there is variation in for *whom*

I do it. Experience also exposes the harsh reality of working in any kind of public service, and even more in God's service, whether I am a teacher or an emergency responder.

You see, when you are a teacher, there is an excuse (to a certain extent) for a teenager to act like a butthead. In the EMS world, (to an extent), there is an excuse for a very ill patient to be cranky. It's easy to want to help the cheery, eager, appreciative people. It takes a little more to help those that are the complete opposite. The world of serving others is funny (by "funny" I mean "mysterious"). Ironically, the tiniest gesture like a smile or sharing a snack, makes you realize how *easy* happiness and peace can be. Those feelings make professions like teaching or being an EMT worthwhile. I believe that these feelings are due to the fact that they are genuine. You may find that simple acts of kindness occur few and far between, and sometimes you must struggle REAL hard to catch and hold onto them. But they are some of the most valuable rewards you will ever receive, and thus, that much more valuable to give.

So, here's the hard part. There is obviously a degree of stress that comes with being a teacher or a first responder. You mentally prepare yourself for those things. However, when you start to see the reality of what being "burnt out" can do to people's attitudes and efforts, well, it's heartbreaking and frustrating. You pray hard, and you push yourself to stay positive because you *know* you have to. Sadly, you realize that there are sometimes situations where you must "play the game" too, in order for you to accomplish your good intentions. Whether you want to call it "business," "politics," or "kissing ass," the game is always around to challenge you to choose between who you are and who you truly desire to become.

I hold tight to my belief that *everybody* has a heart. Let me tell you, sometimes that is the *most exhausting* belief to hold on to. Sometimes I think believing *that* is harder than believing I could win the lottery. But I think it's worth it. Why?

Well, I wouldn't go to church if I were perfect. The reason I have a relationship with God is for the very same reason my relationship with God needs work. See, God is always steady and consistent. No matter how many ways I have been judgmental, selfish, or wrong (especially when I thought I was being selfless doing it!) I can always go back to the Lord feeling crappy and moody. I can curse at him (not that that's a good thing!) because I'm angry or cry to him because I'm sad. But I can and should come to him with a smile and say thanks. If God sent Jesus to set the example for me, I should probably try to follow the example. This brings me back to my EMT job.

Oh, For the Love of God

Throughout completing paramedic school, I was privileged to work and train with a few different companies and organizations in a big city. First, it is important to note that for the record, I know there are first responders who are ridiculously hard-working and have hearts of gold. To you I tip my hat.

On my final day at one particular job, my gut kept reassuring me that resigning from this company was necessary. It was a matter of self-respect. Immediately walking into my first day of that EMT job, I got this feeling that there was a very negative vibe, but I tried to be optimistic. At the same time, I didn't want to appear to be such a new "eager beaver" to the experienced "seasoned" veterans who had worked there for ages. However, I believe there is always room to be civil. Anyone who walked through the station door gave me hope for a helpful coworker to befriend. While there were a handful of friendly folks, most interactions were disheartening.

"Hi," I would say with one of those weird smiles. You know, the kind where you try not to look too excited. You make sure you don't show your teeth and your bottom lip pushes up into your upper lip. As the person approached, I was hoping for any decent response. Eye contact would have been nice, but I usually got nothing. An occasional "Hey" was exciting. Giving people the benefit of the doubt, I assumed they just had a bad day. But that compromising got to be a REALLY old routine. It did not take long to admit to myself that no one gave a crap about me or worse, about *anything*. As the naive newbie I was determined to NOT develop that attitude for myself or toward others. But it's hard to keep your focus and surround yourself with good company when you are, well, not surrounded by good company and possibly stuck with that company for anywhere from 4 to 24-hour shifts.

Anytime I would be partnered with an experienced employee, I tried to make the most of it, whether it was by trying to have a decent conversation or trying to at least learn something about the job. At this point, I did not need a friend, I just needed less bad vibes. The way I saw it, if I might one day be stuck with you for hours as a partner, I had to make it tolerable.

"So, you're the new EMT huh?" was often the phrase I heard with each new partner I was with.

Boy, I wanted to jump up and hug any partner who talked to me. But you know, you play it cool.

"Yeah, just getting started," I would casually reply trying to stay cool. "You?" I'd remind myself just keep looking out the window, like I was not excited.

"Oh, been here 'bout 12 years or so."

"Nice," I would say. Despite the variation in years that every new partner provided, they all followed up with the same statement.

"Yeah," they would say, "this place is a good place to get started, but I wouldn't work here long." My face would go back to that weird smile I described pushing my lower lip up, and I replied with a "Heh." So much for conversation. My focus went back to my phone and scrolling on Facebook.

"God I hope we have a lot of patients to get to," I thought, *"because if not, then I'm going to be wasting another several hours with this bundle of joy sitting next to me."* I wished that my partner would just drive by my apartment and I would gladly jump out.

It was simple. I was not happy. I *just* left a different career to get out of a negative environment, and I wasn't about to put myself through that again. I told myself to first give it a chance. Maybe I just needed to get the hang of things and get to know co-workers. What's my motto? No regrets. The patients I were called to help had not done anything to me. So, I gave everything I had as best as I could to this job and to the patients who needed my help. I find that giving your best in anything you do makes it easier to come to terms with walking away from your circumstances. The more you catch yourself struggling to give your best, the more you understand that you need to step back and re-examine yourself.

When you give your best, it makes it less scary to admit that you must make a change for yourself. You never have to walk away thinking "What if..." or "If I just..."

* * *

So, here I was, on a chilly December day that would be my last day with that EMT job. One of our calls was not an emergency call, but instead a simple transport of a patient from a hospital to an assisted living facility. You never knew the whole story of the patient, simply the time and location of pick-up and drop-off. My partner and I arrived at the hospital and checked in at the nurses station. The patient's room was at the end of the hall, but we waited because the nurse had to finalize some preparation for transport (paperwork, administer medication, and so on). I saw that there were a few of people waiting around outside the room, wandering in and out. I rolled the stretcher to put it out of the way against the wall, and just hung out waiting. After a few minutes, a middle-aged man walked toward us.

"Hi," he said. "Are you all going to be transporting my mother?"

"Yes, sir," my partner and I replied. This man began to tell us a bit about his mother and he looked a bit uneasy.

"We all just learned that mom probably only has a little bit of time to live," he said.

"*Whoaaa, did not expect that.*" I thought to myself. "Oh wow. I'm sorry to hear that," I said. "Yeah, sorry to hear that," my partner said.

The man sighed. "Yes, well, she has been battling cancer among some other things for a good while. I just wanted y'all to know that she might not be in the best of moods when you see her." Well, gee. What do you say to that? I felt bad. Hell of a last day on the job! I was a little bit familiar with how this guy felt, having spent time with my mom in home hospice, but for some reason, I didn't want to tell him that. While my intentions would have been to show empathy, I worried that sharing my story may come off as "comparing" stories. I know that if I'm talking to someone in search of support, the last thing I want to hear is anything that remotely sounds like "my story is better (meaning worse than) than your situation." So, I quietly gave a sideways smile.

"We understand," I said. "But I'm glad you are able to visit her, and I'm sure she is too." That was the best reply I could think of. A few other short words were awkwardly exchanged among the three of us, and the man made his way back to the room.

I stood there waiting quietly and trying to think of general, pleasant conversation I might be able to make with the family and patient. I also thought it would be a great time to offer comfort in God. I knew that that kind of conversation must be done with tact, confidence, and all around carefully, especially when you don't know the other person. I have no fear in wanting to share my faith. It's always just a matter of how to bring it into a conversation or situation.

Anyway, as I stood around thinking and looking at posters on the wall, I looked up and saw the man coming back toward us. I gave a little smile and so did he. He walked up to my partner and put in his hand some money, a tip.

"Here," he said as he stuffed it into my partner's hand, almost as if to do it secretively. "It's a thank you for what you guys do, and to make sure you get my mom comfortably and safely to the facility."

It was literally a two-minute transport across the street from the hospital. My partner and I both said we could not take the money. "Driving the ambulance is part of our job," my partner said, "Don't worry about it." I nodded.

The man insisted. We went back and forth a few times, the man trying real hard to put the money in my partner's hand. At some point, I think my partner and I looked at each other and kind of laughed. We felt like it would be an insult to this guy if we didn't take the money. So, my partner took it, then the man came over and placed a folded up bill in my hand, patted me on the shoulder with a friendly smile, and walked back to the room. My partner and I said thanks, just kind of looked at each other, sort of laughed, and looked down at our hands. I expected a wad of ones or maybe a $5 bill, but instead found a $20 bill. To me, that was a heck of a tip! I tried my best to control my facial expression. I looked at my partner and by the look on his face he was a bit taken aback as well. Then, all of a sudden, I remembered the two $20 bills I had kept from two previous Christmases. That was two years ago. *"I'll be darned,"* I thought. Was it a coincidence it always happened around Christmas, and it always happened while I struggled with a career change? I guess God loves to make sure I remember what's important in every step I take no matter where I am in life. I recalled that promise to myself - to never put myself in a bad financial position again and to appreciate what I have, be it possessions or opportunities.

That moment of waiting while leaning against the stretcher, I felt like no matter what happened after today, everything was going to be ok. Despite the disappointment of yet another job change, I found comfort and reassurance reminding myself that this was my situation because I refused to just settle. I'm a "go-getter." While I promised to dig myself out of a shaky financial situation two years ago, I stood there and laughed to myself, *"Well, shit. I'm actually doing even worse money and job-wise two years later!"* All I could do was nod my head back and forth and roll my eyes while smiling to myself. Somehow, I felt like I was still on the right path and that encouragement was not because of my nice little monetary tip. It was because of the situation I was in when I received the money.

My partner drove the ambulance, and I sat in the back with the patient. To be honest, transporting went just fine with no complications and only general conversation. My goal was to simply be pleasant, friendly, and smile. And that's all I did. Honestly, I don't remember what I said on the ride over. I suppose the Holy Spirit took over because first of all, the patient was quite pleasant, and I remember she even had a bit of a sense of humor. Within 15 minutes of working to load the patient we were already at the facility helping our patient settle in. As my partner and I were transferring her to her bed, she gently smiled at us.

"You guys are great," she said.

My partner jokingly smiled and said, "Yeah, tell that to my partner here," he nodded toward me. "She's a traitor. Today is her last day working with us."

The patient looked over to me and said, "Oh, really? That's too bad. You're wonderful."

"Thank you," I was a little embarrassed. "But yes, ma'am, today is my last day." I started to help fix the sheets and pull the blanket up around her on the bed.

There was an awkward silence and I felt like I was supposed to say more, like everyone in the room was waiting for me to explain why I was leaving. I smiled and with my voice slightly cracking, I said the first thing I could think of.

"I think it's just about that time for me to go, you know? To move on." I gently smiled while I pulled the rail back up on the stretcher and looked up.

"Absolutely," our patient smiled back.

"Y'all have a great day and God bless," I said as my partner and I started to move the stretcher out of the room.

"Thank y'all so much," the family said to us. I kept smiling and walking while swallowing down a huge lump in my throat. Looking back, I think it was appropriate to say. Although there was sadness in the air, I feel like it was filled with peace, for both my patient and for myself. Moving on sounded nice.

That day I was a hot mess of anxious and sad about a lot of things. I often thought about my mom and wondered if she would be proud of me even if I hadn't quite settled in a career yet. Oddly enough, I knew in my heart that the new job I had lined up was not going to be much better. The only difference was the name of the company. But I told myself it would be some improvement, and more importantly, another step on my journey. That $20 bill told me to move on without worry because God would provide as long as my path focuses on HIS will. As crazy as my journey has been, not once have I been homeless, not once have I had nothing to eat. I thought of a little poster I was given by the Sisters of St. Joseph while I was a teacher in Rochester, New York. The words on the small white poster were written in bright colors.

"Saint Joseph found his life in ordinary days-no clutter of 'if's or buts' – simply in what we call now."

God will throw you into some crazy mess if you let him. But that is the key—to let him. And while you are there, you must trust and do what is right. You must treat others kindly no matter how difficult. You must realize that you must work and realize that work comes in many different forms. It might mean completing a task in front of you or it could mean taking steps to improve who you are as a person. In that time, if faith in God's will serves as your motivation you *will* make it. God provides what you NEED at the time, not what you WANT. With that belief, you will discover that wherever God leads you, it is in fact where you need to be. So just do it for the love of God.

* * *

Looking back, I see that leaving that particular job and moving on only allowed me to strive to become a better person. On my last day working I was reminded in a variety of ways, about the importance of staying focused on my true purpose - to serve in whatever situation I find myself in life. As I drove home from work that night, I drove away with an odd sense of relief. Barely a quarter of a mile from the ambulance station and getting set to merge onto I-45 to head home, I had one of those famous talks with myself.

"Focus, Nicole, make it home safely. Just focus on the road."

I expected it to be difficult to drive. But no matter how hard I tried, I didn't feel like crying. It was almost as if I was *fighting* myself because I *was* focused!

"*Hmm,*" I thought "*Maybe emotions would kick in in a few minutes. You know, like you're in shock and it takes a moment.*" I waited. Nothing. The only feeling creeping up was exhaustion.

"I'm tired, *always* tired, Lord." I started to ask God, "Can you PLEASE just help me finally settle into some kind of decent job, even just for a few years?" For a moment, I thought something was wrong with me. I tried to feel sad, but I started to realize that my lips were slowly curving up. I had a smile on my face.

"No, never mind, God. No more settling for me," I said to myself. "Let's get somewhere first. You just gotta help me get there. Got it? Just help me get there. Please."

I was proud of myself for finally taking care of myself. Respecting myself felt pretty darn good, and for once, letting go of people who aren't nice became a lot easier. Being in negative work environments took its toll on me, but it also helped me learn to take pride in who I knew I wanted to be, and how much potential I had to be a better person. I had only a slight idea of what I was about to get myself into, but I knew it was the right direction.

Just Move the Chains

I'm probably not the inventor of this analogy, but it clicked in my brain one Sunday while watching a football game.

I like to think of life as a football game. I want to go all the way to the endzone for a touchdown (in my case settling into a great career and life), but it isn't always about running a hundred yards on the first try. It is about continuously pushing forward. It's also realizing that other people are trying to get to an endzone, and they may reach it before you. It's not your turn...yet. Many times, the game is defense, and you must protect your side when necessary. When it is your turn, some plays you will lose yards; some plays you make huge gains, and some only a few inches. However, sometimes a few inches are all it takes to move the chains forward for the first down. With that, comes more chances to score a touchdown. If you can just keep moving the chains with a first down, the endzone will eventually appear.

As I was getting ready for bed that same night, the words finally came out of my mouth.

"This is stupid!" I was still worried that I had not felt worried enough. "I give up! I don't even know what I'm giving up on. But I give up." I realize now that I gave up on trying so hard to find my place and just take it in stride (with purpose, of course).

I began to think about the day I just had. I decided even if I got into a financial hole again, I would *not* spend that $20 tip. It had more worth than the face value. Receiving that tip somehow tugged me back on track. It reminded me to never forget the importance of living out your most basic, yet most powerful faith at *all* times. My EMT career was short-lived, but it held very important opportunities to be a part of pivotal points in the lives of other human beings. Being present and bringing all of myself to the job was more important than any employer's job description. I wasn't where I thought I should be in life, but shame on me for thinking

I was deserving of more. I am always simply where God needs me.

In three years I saved up the most valued $60 in my life, and that money still sits in the same box. But it all came down to a few things. It is about sticking to priorities. It's about following values. It's about working hard and then letting God put the rest together.

10

The End . . . Sort Of

✌

I really can't figure out how to end this book, and I think it's because *my* story hasn't actually *ended.* It has been an everchanging work in progress. Let me tell you, I can silently be the most competitive, determined little sucker, and I think God is onto me. On my most disheartening and demoralizing days, God tells me to shut up by either humbling me or by stirring up my soul with frustration. Either way, it points me toward a greater purpose to serve and while I cannot put an exact description to this purpose, some days it just feels like I catch a tiny feeling of it and it sure is beautiful. Trust me, you know it when you feel it simply because it's *not* tangible.

Like anyone else, I set my goals and I have my dreams. I will not give up because I'm stubborn, or as I like to call it – strong-willed. Whatever I get caught up in now is nothing new to any adult—that balance of keeping that dream alive and paying the bills. It's not easy, and THANK GOD I have people willing to help me along the way. God provides through our hands and feet. It's not always God parting the sea or "making" me win the lottery (but I won't reject it if he gives it to me!). However, as they say, it's all about the journey. I've done a lot, and I am still young. None of my teaching career, martial arts programs, or emergency response career, came close to what I had imagined. But you know what? I did it. The experiences taught me incredible lessons and I had fun. I feel like through my pursuits I may have helped people gain their confidence and find moments of silliness, joy, or peace. I realize there were moments I found the same benefits for myself.

My saved stash of $20 bills reminds me that no matter what gripes I have, I must see each day as an opportunity. Life is a journey, and each day is a step. We have all heard that, and we all know it. Now go and live it. I won't be the first or the last to complain that it's a long journey! But again, if the good Lord gets me up each day, then there is work for me to do and I need to report for duty. Maybe it's better if I'm a *little* bit unsure about what I'm getting into, then I'm not limited by my own plans. I think I've learned that nothing works out the way I plan anyway!

Truth be told, I may become a little lost, tired, and sometimes discouraged. Although I'm very often *frustrated,* somehow, it is rare that I worry. No matter how much I plan and try to make informed decisions and moves, only God knows where each step will take me. But my friends, and to my readers, here is to moving on! And here is to those who help along the way.

I heard somewhere that God will sometimes isolate you to help you realize that he is all you need, that being *away* from people and things that often have the most influence on you (even if it is a good influence), is what helps you better understand whatever God is ready for you to learn in life. Truth be told, with each new career I tried, I felt like I was stepping further and further away from who I believed myself to be. Often it has been an isolated journey for me. The further away I got from who I thought I was, the closer I got to who I think I will be happier being. And most of all, the closer I got to God. Truly a haphazard, serendipitous Easter egg hunt.

I often go back to what my mom said. *"You have to pray. You have to have faith. If you work hard and do right, God is always on your side, so there is no need to be scared."*

You know, I didn't succeed in a lot of things, but I don't think I ever truly failed, simply because I put so much into everything I try. No regrets.

I believe there is good (and not so good) still to come. I think that miracles are often the things that happen while you sort through ambitions and work to get to what you *think* is the miracle. The miracle you *expect* may or may not happen. If you keep your eyes and mind open and are willing to get your hands dirty, parts of your journey reveal tons of miracles and in forms you never would have imagined. Sometimes it even takes a few years to recognize they happened. And even *more* beautiful, as my friend Al outside of Starbucks showed me, sometimes what feels like your hardships are actually miracles for others. I mean, who helped who between Al and me? We both thought we were losing at life. God's plan is *not* always *your* miracle. If your hardships become someone else's miracle, well goodness, how much more proof do you need that God finds your life worth more than you realize? Live to help others, and God will make you the answer to someone's prayers! Talk about serendipity!

Now, to put my money where my mouth is (but not my beloved $60!), I'll turn forward and keep running the race before me. I encourage you to do the same, no matter how great or miserable you see your life right now. It is time to get back to work for God. Your prize

Easter eggs are laid out every day you wake up. Run, run, run!!

As baseball player turned evangelist Billy Sunday said, *"Stopping at 3rd base adds no more to the score than striking out. It doesn't matter how well you start if you fail to finish."* I have to say I feel like this inning is going on forever. But I'll let God decide when it's over. And, whenever I'm not sure what direction I'm going, I'll just keep telling myself that I'm just trying to get to Heaven.

NOTES

Introduction

1. Bruce Lee, *Striking Thoughts: Bruce Lee's Wisdom for Daily Living* (North Clarendon, VT: Tuttle Publishing, 2000), p.xvii.

Chapter 2

1. Hebrews 11:1. *
2. Matthew 10:14. *

Chapter 3

1. Bruce Lee, *Striking Thoughts: Bruce Lee's Wisdom for Daily Living* (North Clarendon, VT: Tuttle Publishing, 2000), p.5.

Chapter 4

1. Matthew 18:12-14. *

Chapter 5

1. Daniele Bolelli, *On the Warrior's Path: Philosophy, Fighting, and Martial Arts Mythology (2nd ed)* (Berkely, CA: Blue Snake Books, 2008), p.35.

Chapter 6

1. website: http://onlineslangdictionary.com/meaning-definition-of/pucker-factor

Chapter 7

1. Ecclesiastes 3:1, 2, 3, 4, 7 *

2. Ecclesiastes 3:12 *

Chapter 8

1. C.S. Lewis, *Mere Christianity* (New York, NY: HarperOne, 2001), p.155

2. Hebrews 12:1, 2, 3, 7, 11-13 *

3. Catholic Church, *Catechism of the Catholic Church* (New York: Doubleday, 1995), 1.

*Scripture texts in this work are taken from the *New American Bible, revised edition* ©1986 Confraternity of Christian Doctrine, Washington, D.C. and are used by permission of the copyright owner. All Rights Reserved. No part of the New American Bible may be reproduced in any form without permission in writing from the copyright owner.

CPSIA information can be obtained
at www.ICGtesting.com
Printed in the USA
LVHW040903150621
690250LV00006B/416

9 781716 059926